THE ROAD TO ZERO
Somalia's Self-Destruction

MOHAMED OSMAN OMAR

THE ROAD
TO ZERO

Somalia's Self-destruction

Personal Reminiscences

HAAN Associates
1992

Published in 1992 by
HAAN Associates
PO Box 607, LONDON SW16 1EB

ISBN 1 874209 75 8

Front cover map drawn by Shannan
Mohamed Abdu Hag

Reprinted 1993

Typeset in Century 10/12pt by Scriptmate
Editions

Printed in Great Britain by The Ipswich Book Company Ltd.

Sources which have been consulted in the
preparation of this book are referenced in
footnotes on the appropriate text pages.

The photographs are reproduced from the
following sources: *Somali News,*
Mogadishu; the author's personal
photographic collection; Mogadishu from
the Air Calendar 1986, USAID, Mogadishu,
Somalia; Somalia National Film Agency;
UN Archives.

DEDICATED TO
THE SOMALI PEOPLE

'Hal bacaad lagu lisey'
A camel milked onto the sand has all its efforts dissipated
SOMALI PROVERB

Acknowledgements

First and foremost, I am indebted to my family and relatives who have patiently borne with me during the course of my professional career, which provides the setting for my narration. I am also beholden to those of my friends who gave me continuous encouragement to write these few lines. I was born in Mogadishu in 1937, and my lifetime has spanned five changing and momentous decades in the life of my people and country. My personal reminiscences of living through these decades, being moulded by them, and participating in them as a citizen, government functionary, and diplomat, may strike a chord with others of my countrymen and women who have a story to tell. I hope this may encourage them to make their own contribution to the record for the sake of our succeeding generations.

Most of the chapters of this book were written during the year of civil war in Somalia which followed the ousting from power in January 1991 of Mohamed Siad Barre, and during which my mind was constantly distracted by the daily news of killing and destruction taking place in the country. My thanks to the Diplomatic Staff of the Somali Embassy in New Delhi for their cooperation and support during the period of my writing. My thanks to Mr. I. Edward, my driver, who willingly extended a helping hand to assist with household responsibilities, allowing me enough time to complete the book; I am most grateful to him.

My profound gratitude to Professor Shams-ud-din, School of International Studies, Jawaharlal Nehru University, New Delhi, India, who read through the first draft of my manuscript and gave me some useful suggestions to bring it to shape. My sincere thanks also to Mr. Jagdish Chander Vidyarthi for typing the manuscript, my gratitude to the U.N. Information Center and U.N.I.C.E.F. in New Delhi for their valuable assistance, and last, but not least to my publisher and editor, who has been a friend for more than half the span of years which this book covers. The views and conclusions expressed in the book are attributable only to me.

M.O.O.
New Delhi, July 1992

Contents

LIST OF ILUSTRATIONS opposite page

1. Mogadishu: the Government building on the right of   14
the minaret, and Umberto di Savoia Arch just visible.

2. Abdullahi Issa Mohamud: Prime Minister during the   26
UN Trusteeship 1956-60.

3. National Assembly building.   32

4. Aden Abdulle Osman: First President of the Republic,   50
1960-67.
5. Abdirashid Ali Shermarke: Prime Minister 1960-64,
and President 1967-69.
6. Abdirazak Haji Hussein: Prime Minister 1964-67.
7. Mohamed Haji Ibrahim Egal: Prime Minister 1967-69.

8. The Author as Diplomat in London.   79

9. Major General Mohamed Siad Barre: after staging the   88
coup in 1969.

10. First Charter of the Revolution.   91

11. Second Charter of the Revolution.   92

12. The Supreme Revolutionary Council Members and   95
Civilian Members of the Government, during the early
period.

13. Life-size paintings of Marx, Engels, Lenin and Siad: 113
'Architects of Socialism'.

14. Third Charter of the Revolution.   145

15. The way 'Revolution Day' was celebrated: tight   148
security.

16. Party Members saying "Yes".   151

17. Insignia of the Somali Revolutionary Socialist Party.   158

18. The Author with Tennis Trophy.   180

Preface

Recent developments in Somalia have been a source of anxiety and pain to all Somalis, wherever they may be. Our future is uncertain and bleak. As an independent nation we have collectively failed to establish a political system which could have guaranteed the fundamental right to existence. We have miserably failed to fulfil the basic needs of our people. Perhaps, we devoted too much of our attention and resources to overcoming the disabilities, problems and disputes which we inherited from our colonial masters and which, naturally, led us to involvment in external struggle, giving us no time to consolidate the gains of our national freedom by creating and developing the institutions without which no nation in modern times can survive.

The civil war which is now raging in the country should open our eyes. If we are to learn anything from this event—which has been appropriately described as "a human disaster of the first magnitude"—it must be that we sink our differences and start afresh. If necessary, we should not shy away from accepting advice and the good offices of the United Nations, the O.A.U. (Organization of African Unity), the Arab League, and friendly countries, to put an end to the genocidal conflict which we have been waging upon ourselves.

The world is aghast at the macabre dance being played out in Somalia. Our friends are worried about our continued ability to survive as a nation. But we still seem to be oblivious to the threat.

Somalia was one of the countries that emerged during the sixties as independent states in Africa. Unlike other countries of Africa, Somalia has the distinction of being a homogenous society. Somalis are Muslims and speak the Somali language. It should have been easier for us to consolidate our hard-won freedom had our leaders been a little more sincere and mature and a little less power hungry and selfish.

In the following pages I have made a modest attempt to narrate the story of our country as it has evolved during the preceding four decades. A large part of my narration is based on my personal observations during the years in which I have, in one capacity or the other, been employed in the service of my country.

May Allah help us to resolve our problems and guide us to reconstruct our nation.

Foreword

Both the author and publisher of this book are friends from the pre-Siyadism ultra-liberal times of the Mogadishu of the mid-sixties. The three of us belonged to the extravagantly free budding media of Somalia. Mohamed Osman and Anita Suleiman were crucial officers of SONNA, Somalia's state-owned news agency, and key members respectively of *Il Corriere della Somalia* and the *Somali News,* the Government's Italian and English newspapers. I was the owner-editor of the leading anti-Government periodical of the time, the English language *Dalka*

It is consequently a special pleasure for me to congratulate both the author and publisher of *The Road to Zero.* It is not easy to classify this fine work as a 'modern history of Somalia' or an 'autobiography' or a 'travelogue'. It is much more than 'Reminiscences of a Somali Diplomat'—and not merely because it goes substantially beyond the author's diplomatic assignments. There is first the fact that not many of the Somali diplomats of the era of Siyadism would have the literary ability, or even the literacy, to write such a book. Still fewer would have shown, in recording their experiences, the captivating scruples and honesty manifested by the author throughout this work.

My lauding of the author's scruples and honesty does not mean that I find accurate, or even adequate, all the author's presentations and comments on the events of our recent past. For instance, the author gives the impression that former President Siyad Barre's atrocious State terrorism—founded on the unprecedented use of blatant tribalism while denouncing it with equally unprecedented force—was embarked on only after the 1977 war with Ethiopia. In fact, I myself was among the first 13 victims of Siyadism—specifically selected on tribal criteria and in order to terrorize the people, subjected to dawn arrests for detention at secret locations, indefinitely. That was on 22 April 1970, or exactly six months after the assumption of power by Siyad Barre. Political executions, with or without show trials, were resorted to shortly thereafter.

The author cannot be expected in the circumstances to be aware of the fact that the Issaq of the North had the unwelcome distinction of being the only major clan to be collectively targeted by Siyadism for wholesale persecution; or that they were the only tribal group, at any tribal level, to have remained throughout Siyad Barre's rule a top priority for all the means and methods of maximum persecution. Although the author knew of and makes mention of Siyadism's horrific anti-Issaq atrocities, like the Mogadishu random rounding up of 41 men from their homes, simply on account of their being Issaq, and their mass execution the same night in Jazira beach, he diplomatically ducks identifying them as Issaq.

The above explanatory notes are in no way intended to qualify my admiration for this heart-uplifting book. It is an admirable impressionistic panorama of post-Colonial Somalia. It adds to its patent honesty another equally desirable quality, namely the blessing of readability. Even the young, deprived of adequate familiarity with non-Somali languages by Siyadism's demagogic championing of Somali, should find it approachable.

In this connection, Mohamed Osman repeats the Somalis' near-unanimity of high praise for former President Siyad Barre for his selecting of a script to give the Somali language a written dimension. I beg to differ with this view, and consider that the decision was a national disaster. What is forgotten is that the undoubted richness we do not fail to attribute to our native language applies only to our verbal needs as nomads. Our Somali language is therefore virtually useless for expressing scientific, technical and indeed all abstract conceptions, because we, as nomads, had no use for them. We are all only too familiar with the resulting virtual destruction of the Somali educational system through its adoption as the scholastic medium of instruction.

I repeat, in conclusion, my hearty well-done to the author and the publisher. The individual enterprise shown by both is our sure hope for getting out of the present morass.

YOUSUF DUHUL
London, August 1992

CHAPTER I

Towards Self-Rule

I remember neither the date nor the exact time that I along with some of my classmates happened to be there with our school teacher, Mrs Geeran, a British lady. She took us to a garden, the only garden in the city of Mogadishu. We stood under a huge arch which had been erected in the middle of the garden by the Italian fascists during their colonial rule of that part of the territory.

I stood on Mrs. Geeran's right side. On the other side was her big dog who was always with her when she was not working. I always tried to avoid dogs because I had learnt as a Muslim that the dog is a *nijaas* animal. We were taught that if one touched a dog one must wash oneself seven times in order to be clean again. On that day, like the animal standing there, I did not know why I was there. Of course, I was already going to school, learning to read and write—a good fortune which my father and most people of his age group had not had under the fascist Italian occupation of the country. But my learning was not yet sufficient for me to understand what was happening on that particular day.

My father used to tell me that the Italians, who had ruled the territory for over 50 years, prohibited the people from learning anything. Education was provided only up to the third grade during the later period of colonial rule and in any case there were no schools in the real sense.

Italy had ruled this part of the Somali territories since 1889, up until its defeat by the British forces during the Second World War in 1941. The 1st of April 1950 marked the day Italy was again taking over the administration of ex-Italian Somaliland from the British Military Administration which had been in charge there since 1941. Italy had been designated by the United Nations to prepare the former Italian territory for independence within ten years, and this handing-over was the event I was witnessing. It was in accordance with the U.N. Resolution 289 (IVA) adopted by the General Assembly in its 250th Meeting on 21 November 1949, which among other things stated:

'1. That Italian Somaliland shall be an independent sovereign state;

2. That this independence shall become effective at the end of ten years from the date of the approval of a Trusteeship Agreement by the General Assembly;

3. That, during the period mentioned in paragraph 2, Italian Somaliland shall be placed under the International Trusteeship System with Italy as the Administering Authority'.*

Along with Mrs. Geeran, I looked at the white painted building *Palazzo del Governo* which had been constructed during the Fascist administration and which was the headquarters of the government. It was not as big as *Palazzo Venezia* in *Piazza Venezia* in Rome, but it had a balcony like the one used by the Duce, Benito Mussolini, whenever he wished to address the Italian people.

The building, in the heart of the city of Mogadishu, was meant to accommodate all the government departments. In front of it stood the biggest building in Mogadishu—the Roman Catholic Cathedral, which had been built during the same period, in the 1930s. To the left of the *Palazzo del Governo* stood the only hotel of Mogadishu, the *Croce del Sud* or Southern Cross, also built in the 30s, to accommodate official guests of the Government.

Among those who knew very well what was happening that day were my teacher, the British, Italians, and the members of the UN Advisory team who were standing on the balcony. The Union Jack still flew over their heads. They were ready for the exchange of ownership of my territory, and this was the fourth time in living memory its ownership was being changed.

During the late 19th century the Sultan of Zanzibar had ruled our territory. It had next passed to the Italians who ruled it for more than fifty years. During the Second World War the British defeated Italy and took control, and now another master was taking over in the garb of the United Nations Trusteeship.

* *Yearbook of the United Nations* 1948-49, p276; UN Publications

Mogadishu: the Government building on the right of the minaret, and Umberto di Savoia Arch just visible.

Suddenly there was total silence. It was as if everyone had stopped breathing. The military band, specially dressed for the occasion, was getting ready. Although all of them had their music sheets stuck on their instruments, I am sure they had all learnt by heart the notes they were about to play.

Also getting ready were the ceremonially dressed soldiers who were to offer the salute to the flags—the Union Jack which was to be lowered and the Italian Tricolour which was to be hoisted. My teacher was attempting to explain to me, step by step, what was going on and what it all meant. What I gathered from her explanation was that the moment the Italian Tricolour was hoisted, she and the other British people would leave the country. She was clearly sad because her flag was being lowered, and I felt unhappy and confused. Could a mere change in the colour of the flags make all that difference? I did not want Mrs. Geeran to go, and I did not want my English schooling to end.

During the ten years of British rule in the territory, a programme had been started for the education of the masses. Was there any justification for changing that now? Would continuation of British rule have been a lesser evil than the government that was about to replace it, the government which was the stated preference of our leaders of the time?

This new period of Italian rule would be different from the earlier one which had existed for the 50 years prior to 1941. My father used to tell me stories about the earlier period, when the Italian colonizers tortured, whipped and humiliated the Somalis. There were stories of Somalis being used as a human bridge or sandbank, to enable the Italians to cross rivers, and how some were killed by crocodiles. I also heard tell that one of our neighbours was lashed to death. This new Italian administration, however, got its orders from the new Republic of Italy which had replaced the Fascist regime of Benito Mussolini. The approach and aim of the new authority was different, as was its mandate.

The Commander of the Guard of Honour called his soldiers to attention. The band began playing a tune very familiar to me—the national anthem of the United Kingdom—'God Save the King'.

It was familiar because we used to have to sing its Arabic ver-

sion each time the British District Commissioner visited our
school in Hamar Weyne.

يا ربنا احفظ
س. م. ملكنا
عادل جليل
فليعش ملكنا ذوالهمم
رحيم عادل
مؤيد بالنصر
وعمر طويل

That was before I joined the Hamar Jab Jab School where Mrs.
Geeran was a teacher. The Hamar Weyne school was originally
a private one, organized by the Shanshiya clan, but later it became a Government school. The Italian Administration called it
Scuola Scianscia.

Mrs. Geeran—or was she Miss Geeran, or Geiron—was a tall
heavily built lady. Now she stood motionless, her eyes fixed on
the Union Jack that was being slowly lowered. I looked at her
face and noticed tears trickling down her cheeks. It was the end
of an historic decade. This was the first decade that the Somalis
had had the chance to study. Now teachers like Mrs Geeran were
being asked to pack up and leave the country. As for us, we had to
face the prospect of another system of education.

The British were not our brothers, but they had become a part
of our history, as had the Italians before them, and comparison of
the two is inevitable. From 1889-1941 when Italy ruled the territory there was no positive human, social, educational, or political activity. On the contrary, there had been forcible confiscation
of farmlands, a disregard for human dignity, and total denial of
political freedom.

Compared to this, the ten years of British Military Administration had seen the establishment of schools, an upsurge
in local political activities, and the establishment of nationalist
political parties such as the Somali Youth Club (SYC).

The SYC was founded on 15 May, 1943, and later became the

Somali Youth League (SYL), the dominant pre-independence national party which, still later, formed successive civilian governments in the independent Somali Republic of the 1960s. Of course, this was a period when the attitudes of the colonial powers were being challenged from within and without, and they were being forced to change their ways. This was no doubt a reason why British rule in the 40s appeared much better than the Italian rule people remembered from previous decades, and so it is somewhat surprising that the senior Somali leaders and politicians of the day were not in favour of Britain over Italy as the continuing trusteeship administrator of our country, especially in light of the Bevin Plan.

In 1946 a landmark proposal for the future of the Somalilands was put forward by Britain. The proposal, which came to be known as the Bevin Plan after its architect and staunch advocate, the then Foreign Secretary of Great Britain Ernest Bevin, embraced the concept of a Greater Somalia. According to the plan, the former Italian Somaliland, British Somaliland, the Ogaden and Northern Frontier District (N.F.D.), all of which were at that time under British Military Administration and which constituted about 90 per cent of the Somali territories, were to be brought together in a single unit as a U.N. trusteeship under British administration. The Bevin Plan implied the unity of all Somali territories except the part controlled by France.

The proposal was opposed by the United States of America and the Soviet Union. But Mr. Bevin continued most forcefully to argue for and defend the case for a Greater Somaliland. Elaborating on his plan in the House of Commons in London on 4 June, 1946, in the face of Soviet criticism, he said: '...But what attracted M. Molotov's criticism was, I am sure, that I suggested that Great Britain should be made the administering authority. Was this unreasonable?' He emphasized Britain's knowledge of the Horn, and her role during the War in single handedly defeating Italy in East Africa. 'I hope the deputies at the Paris Conference will now consider a greater Somaliland more objectively,' he continued.

'All I want to do in this case is to give those poor nomads a chance to live. I do not want anything else. We are paying nearly £1,000,000 a year out of our Budget to help to support them....We must consider it objectively. If the Conference do not like our proposal we will not be dogmatic about it; we are prepared to see *Italian Somaliland* (Author's italics) put under the United Nations' trusteeship.' Bevin was prepared to accept only Italian Somaliland under UN supervision. Britain kept the rest of the Somali territories under its control.

It was not clear why the Americans and the Russians opposed the British proposal. Neither had expressed an interest in overseeing the territory or in having a piece of the cake.

Standing under the blue sky of Mogadishu in the centre of the beautiful only garden of the city, my teacher took out her handkerchief and wiped the tears from her face. Her eyes behind her spectacles were red. Her sadness transferred itself to me.

The Italian flag was hoisted and a new era was to begin. Mrs. Geeran would leave the country and the English books would be thrown away. The newcomers would bring text-books with similar alphabets, but different pronunciation. Italian geography and history would be taught.

I had no power or say in the matter. All I could do was just watch what was happening.

By the end of the decade of British Military Administration the political parties were already in high gear. The Somali Youth League was the leading party and its influence had spread throughout the Somali territories under British rule in a relatively short period of time.

The political parties, and members of the Somali Youth League in particular, should have known what was in our interest, and which colonial power would have been most useful to our cause. The SYL slogan was "Unity of all Somali Territories." The implementation of the Bevin Plan was exactly what every Somali would have loved to see.

The SYL had been successful in mobilizing the whole Somali nation and Somali people everywhere, right up to Harar. Political representatives were sent to the United Nations in New York to present our case before the world body. So, what had gone wrong? Why had we lost the chance to move along the road to fulfilling our national aspirations? Why were we being divided up once again?

Though the political parties were still young, the politicians were old enough and seasoned enough to know that the unity and independence of the country were the uppermost considerations in everybody's mind.

Towards the end of the 1940s, the Somali Youth League's mobilization of the masses led to the uprisings known as *Dhagaxtuur* (stone-throwing) and Ha Noolaato (long-life-to), which signaled to the colonial powers the people's determination to press for freedom and self-rule. The signals did not fall on deaf ears. In 1948, a United Nations Four-Power Commission, consisting of the United States of America, the Soviet Union, Great Britain and France, came to Somalia to ascertain the wishes of the people.

This was a crucial moment for the people of all the Somali territories—the 90 per cent under British rule and the 10 per cent under French administration. The destiny of the territories and the people was in the hands of the politicians who would represent the case on behalf of the people. Their responsibility was very great. They had to assemble and study the range of sentiments that was being expressed by the various representatives of the people, and from organizations such as religious groups which played (and still play) an important role in our society.

Since the British proposal for Greater Somaliland had been opposed by the United States and the Soviet Union in 1946, the United Nations came to the conclusion that the Commission should only discuss the future of former Italian Somaliland which, in effect, meant Balkanization of the territories.

Keeping the territories together depended entirely on the wisdom and skill of those of our politicians who were meeting the Commission. Their ability in arguing the case would be crucial in deciding the fate of the people. In the event, the Commission came to the country and met the leaders of the political parties. The then President of the SYL, Haji Mohamed Hussein is quoted as telling the UN Commission: 'When we [the SYL Executive Committee] saw this [Bevin's statement on Greater Somaliland] being uttered by a Foreign Minister of a great power, we were very happy indeed because it is one of our great aims.'*

However, despite this valuable piece of ammunition in its ar-

---

*   *Somali Nationalism* by Saadia Touval, p80; Harvard Press 1963.

moury, the SYL did not argue in favour of Britain administering the territories; and instead they opted for UN Trusteeship status for the South, which left the rest of the Somalilands with Britain. The SYL was the most important nationalist party and was in the strongest position to influence the outcome of the meetings.

The other party to meet the Commission made its point very clear. The HDMS (Hizbia Dastur Mustaqil Somali, then called by its tribal name Hizbia Dighil e Mirifle), joined in forming the Somalia Conference—a convention of associations—and demanded that the territory be placed under Italian Trusteeship.* This view was vehemently opposed by the Somali Youth League. The demand of the HDMS was unequivocal. Its leaders alone can justify their reasons for such a stand.

At the United Nations, during the discussions in the First Committee from 6 April to 13 May 1949, representatives of two political parties and organizations qualified to speak for the inhabitants of the territory were heard by the Committee:

'THE SOMALI YOUTH LEAGUE favoured collective trusteeship under the United Nations for a period of not more than ten years. Vigorous opposition was recorded to any form of Italian administration.

'THE SOMALI CONFERENCE AND THE PROGRESSIVE LEAGUE OF MIJERSTEIN (sic.) expressed a desire for complete independence, but agreed that the territory was not yet ready for self-government and it was therefore prepared to accept a United Nations Trusteeship, with Italy as the Administering Authority.'**

The Italian Government viewpoint, expressed by Count Sforza, was that Italy was prepared to accept administration of the territory in accordance with terms established by the UN.

Again later in the year 1949, representatives of political parties and organizations, heard by the First Committee upon recommendation of Sub-Committee 16, advised as follows:

'THE SOMALI CONFERENCE—Assurance was given that there would be full adherence to any resolutions adopted by the

*   IBID. p 96
**   *Yearbook of the United Nations 1948-9,* p259; UN Publications

United Nations. Independence was asked for within the time limit strictly necessary to assure a wise administration and stable democratic liberties. It was stated that although the Somali people regarded liberty and freedom as highly desirable, they were not yet ready for absolute independence and would favour a period of United Nations Trusteeship with Italy as the Administering Authority. The Somali Youth League was denounced as an extremist and terrorist organization.

THE SOMALI YOUTH LEAGUE AND HAMAR YOUTH CLUB—The representatives denounced the so-called Bevin-Sforza Agreement and asked for immediate independence. They expressed a willingness to accept a United Nations Trusteeship for an interim period of short duration but were opposed to any form of foreign rule, particularly Italian administration. It was observed that demonstrations had already been staged in protest against proposals concerning the return of Italian administration to Somaliland, and it was intimated that further disturbances might follow.'*

So, what was happening around me on 1 April, 1950 was the implementation of the United Nations General Assembly Resolution passed on 21 November 1949, approving a UN Trusteeship, administered by Italy under a UN Advisory Council, to prepare the former Italian territory for the status of a sovereign African state within a period of ten years.

From that moment, we started Italianizing everything, from coffee-shop menus to the judicial system.

The UN Advisory Council was composed of Colombia, Egypt and the Philippines. But Italy, nominated to administer the territory, had the real executive powers.

---

*   IBID, p268

CHAPTER II

Preparations for Independence

From 1 April 1950, we had AFIS—*Amministrazione Fiduciaria Italiana della Somalia*—which taught us how to be teachers, accountants, typists, bankers, doctors, nurses, directors, and how to man the police, the army, the security corps...

The Somali language did not then have a script. It was spoken but not written. We were an oral society. The poets and singers did not write their songs and poems. They only memorized what they composed. Messages, information akin to letters, were sent through a person who could memorize the whole content, and would travel to another town or village to deliver messages verbally, word for word, as they had been given. Replies were sent in the same way. We did not have a written form for our language. In education and for written communication it was necessary to use a foreign language.

Now that Mrs Geeran and what she represented had gone, and the English language was buried, we began learning everything over again, in Italian. All office correspondence was now to be in Italian. And we were in a hurry, because in ten years time we had to be able to run our country.

Ten years was not, after all, a long time. The Italian administration proceeded to establish all kinds of schools, regular schools in the morning and schools for adults in the afternoon. AFIS brought in teachers from Italy except for Arabic teachers who were brought from Libya, another ex-Italian colony. As a Muslim people, it was traditional for Somalis to learn Arabic. We had always begun learning the Koran at an early age, whether or not we went to formal school.

The Central Bank of Italy, *Banca d'Italia,* opened a branch in Mogadishu. *Banco di Roma* and *Banco di Napoli* quickly followed suit. We continued using the shilling as currency, but in all other respects, we were becoming like a small province of Italy, with all things being done the Italian way.

Some time in 1954, several Somali students, myself among them, were selected to work for the statistics department of the central administration on a part-time basis, to help conduct a population census. The Chief of the department was an Italian. He lectured us for a few days before sending us to various parts of the city. He told us how the city was divided and where each of us should go. He told us not to enumerate the Indian families. He did not say why, but I thought it was perhaps because the Indians did not like other people visiting their homes.

The Chief also told us that we would be paid 75 cents for compiling each family sheet. That was less than one shilling. There were 100 cents to the shilling, and at that time 75 cents could buy a lot. The pay was a good incentive for us to work hard and to fill up more sheets.

For most of us, it was the first time we were being paid for work. I think it was also the first time a census was undertaken. Like everything else at this moment in time, the job was to be finished very quickly.

Off we went! We went from house to house to record the people, the property, the house plan, number of bedrooms, latrines etc. We did not like big families because it took us too much time to fill in their forms. Bachelor households were best for us because we put only one person's name on the sheet and were paid the same amount of money.

In the evenings we returned to the office of the Director, which was situated in a sports club known as *Circolo della Vela,* to hand over the sheets we had duly filled in during the day, and receive our remuneration.

I was doing very well with the people I was enumerating because they were from my own neighbourhood of Hamar Weyne, the oldest part of the city of Mogadishu and still carrying the original, indigenous name of the city—Hamar. In Hamar Weyne people did not talk to strangers and people from outside the group, let alone answer questions relating to their properties and families. They believed that if the Government knew what assets they had, it would come and take them away. I had to explain to them that whatever was being asked concerned the census and nothing else. But I was one of them, and I had their confidence, so I did not have much difficulty getting them to cooperate.

One evening, I returned from the city as usual to deliver the papers and collect my money. The Chief, who went through each form to see if there were any points that required further clarification, lifted his reading glasses and told me, "You are suspended. Tomorrow you will not be working".

I was crestfallen. I asked myself, 'Why?' After all, I had by then acquired good experience and I knew the job was not yet over.

He said angrily, "I told you from the beginning that no one was to visit Indians. No one should register Indians."

That was true. He had said so, but he had not told us why, and had left us to assume the reasons for ourselves. The Indians were even more reluctant to interact with strangers than were the Hamaris. But the area where the Indians lived was my neighbourhood, and in my over-zealousness I had been determined to show the Italian supervisor that I could gain their trust and could persuade them to respond to the questionnaire.

I tried to defend myself. "But this family are my neighbours, and I knew they wouldn't say 'no' when I knocked at their door." The Chief insisted, however, that no matter how they behaved, Indians were Indians, and I should not have registered them in the census.

"All right, if you say so," I said and left, puzzled by his anger and violent reaction, and not understanding why all the inhabitants of the city, including Indians, should not be counted. Anyhow, I must have been doing something right, because two days later, he sent someone to find me, and asked me to start work again, though he could not resist warning me, 'for the last time', that I should not visit any Indian.

In this part of the Somali territory, we could see which way our future was heading. But we did not know in which direction our brothers were heading, the Somalis from whom we had lately been severed, either by mistake or ignorance or by intention, and who were administered by a different colonial power from ourselves. If only Britain had been nominated by the Somali politicians of the time as the administering power, most of the Somali territories could even then have been brought together, united as one, with a good chance in due course of ultimately regaining our brothers who were then under French rule.

All government departments had an Italian expert whose job it was to teach his Somali counterpart how to manage the office, so that he might take over when independence came. This also applied to the armed forces—the *Carabinieri* (police), *Esercito Nazionale* (national army) and *Marina* (navy)—each of which was trained on the Italian model. Regarding the economy too, AFIS paid the salaries and imported spaghetti. Though it should be said they imported rice, also. On the home front, being a country with abundant livestock, meat was readily available in the market. Vegetables and tropical fruits like banana, papaya and grapefruit, grown in Afgoi were transported 27 kilometers to the capital, every morning.

After finishing the census job I got some kind of permanent employment in the Post Office. I passed a simple test of writing, reading and numbers. In the Post Office too, each section was headed by an Italian, and we were to be groomed to replace them.

The year was 1955. The Cashier at the Post Office was an Italian. So was the Controller, while the rest of the Cash section employees were Somalis. I started work at the counter where national and overseas postal orders were handled. Overseas postal orders were available for Italy only. The customers of this service were primarily Italians who had been brought to the country as civil servants or as members of the armed forces, and whose families were in Italy. The service was also used by Italian businessmen who sent money to companies or their families. Ordinary postal orders were used within the territory of Somalia Italiana. There was also another category—Service postal orders—used for the salaries of Government employees in the interior areas of the territory.

On 12 October 1954, the sky-blue flag with its five-pointed star was hoisted aloft. In 1956, six years of Italian Administration, the country was given internal self-rule. Abdullahi Issa Mohamud, a widely respected politician, and leader of the SYL was appointed Prime Minister, with an all-Somali cabinet of ministers.

Abdullahi Issa Mohamud:
Prime Minister during the UN Trusteeship 1956-60.

As in every other department, the Post Office had its Somali co-director who was in training to take the place of an Italian. This process was known as *Somalizzazione*. The Italians had to complete the job of Somalization by the UN's designated target date for independence at the end of the decade. The system of training became like learning to drive without knowing the functioning of the engine, or like sitting beside the driving instructor and merely being shown how to hold the steering wheel.

If the Italians were in a hurry to complete the job of Somalization, so were we. We were very hungry for power. We wanted to see ourselves sitting on the chair of the boss. We wanted to ring the bell to call the messenger. We imagined ourselves as directors, walking down the corridors of ministry buildings with files under our arms and with people stepping aside as we swept past, then falling in step behind us.

Once a colleague of mine paid a postal order of Sh.4,000 to someone who showed him an identity card. A few days later, the bonafide owner came to enquire about the postal order. On checking, it was found that the money had already been paid out. The Post Office informed the police that the man who had encashed the money had presented the identity card of a policeman. The police investigation revealed that the owner of the card was not in Mogadishu on the day the postal order was cashed. Nothing more could be done. The money was lost. The Post Office had to compensate the real owner of the money, and my colleague who had paid the false claimant was ordered to pay back monthly installments of 40 shillings to the Post Office from his salary until the entire amount was recovered.

The case somehow came to be known in the Prime Minister's office, and the Prime Minister, Abdullahi Issa, was moved to take action to protect public money and, by extension, private money. He sent out a written order that any person who was due to receive money, besides being required to show an Identity Card must also affix his or her fingerprint.

The trainee-Director at the Post Office did his rounds from time to time, to see what the people were doing, but he did not really know what was going on, nor did he need to. He was going to be a Director, so all he would need to do would be to put his signature to letters after the Italian secretary had prepared them for him. He found that the majority of the staff at the front desks were Hamari people of Mogadishu. It was clear he did not like this, and would have wished the office to acquire 'new faces'. One day, a well-dressed Somali came to the counter.

"I am expecting some money to arrive from Italy," he said.

I searched for and found his postal order *vaglia internazionale* and asked him to sign for it. Then I pushed the stamp pad towards him and asked him to put his thumbprint on the paper.

"*Mamma Mia*," he shouted at the top of his voice, "I am Doctor So-and-So. I've studied for twenty years and you ask me to put my thumb mark."

At this, a colleague at the far end of the office called out to me that he knew the gentleman and could stand surety for him. I asked my colleague not to intervene.

"I am not going to put my thumbprint," he insisted, adding, "Even Abdullahi Issa can't tell me to do such a thing."

I explained to him that we handled a lot of money and were trying to protect his as well as other people's money, "And if you want to know, this order is from Abdullahi Issa himself," and I showed him the letter signed by the Prime Minister.

Doctor So-and-So had recently returned from Italy where he had studied Law. He would certainly soon start practicing as a lawyer, and in the future he might easily become a Minister or a Judge. Nevertheless, at this moment he was unwilling to show respect either for the rules or for his own Prime Minister.

Another day, a man in police uniform came in with a postal order which he wanted to cash, and I asked him to show me his identity card. He became furious. He said, "Don't you see my uniform?"

"Yes," I said, "but suppose someone stole your uniform from your house and came to me dressed in it and asked for this money to be given to him, should I give it without asking for identification, just because he's dressed up as a policeman?"

The man became even more angry and left the counter.

At 11.30 a.m. when I closed the counter, a policeman was waiting for me in the corridor and told me that I was wanted at the police station. I first reported this to my Chief and then went to the police station. I was taken to an office where an Inspector was waiting for me. I was seated on a chair in front of his desk. He got up from his chair and started pacing the room.

"You Hamaris," he began, "we have brought you independence and you humiliate a policeman in uniform." The Inspector must have forgotten that it was a Hamari, Haji Mohamed Hussein, the then leader of the SYL who in the late 1940s, when Somlia's future was being discussed by the UN, had taken a strong stand for only a limited period of trusteeship and had totally rejected that it be administered by Italy. Likewise, the Hamar Youth Club had taken a vigorous nationalist position in its meetings with the UN committees in the same period.

I should explain that just as 'Hamar' is the local name for Mogadishu, 'Hamari' means a native of Mogadishu. It is like saying *Napolitano, Romano* or *Siciliano* in Italian, and can mean simply that—a person who belongs to a particular place. But if it is intended as abuse, it can also have that connotation. As the Inspector continued to speak, he looked at the walls, never at me. I found his conduct very threatening, and felt nervous. I tried to explain that I had asked for the policeman's identity card to protect the money, his money, everybody and anybody's money.

After a while, he sat down and said, "Even Abdullahi Issa cannot ask such a thing. I will soon come to the Post Office myself, and we will see."

I answered him quietly *"Insha'Allah."* Then he let me go.

This was the second time I had been told 'even Abdullahi Issa cannot...', first by a lawyer, then by a police inspector. One of them was supposed to defend justice, the other was supposed to enforce the laws of the land and protect life and property. Well, such people would soon be playing important and vital roles in our society!

Just as he had said, the Inspector came to the post office. He came with a postal order to cash. That day I was at another counter dealing with foreign Postal Orders. He presented himself to my colleague. He was wearing his police inspector's uniform with a short thin black baton under his arm.

"Can you please show me your Identity Card," asked my colleague.

The Inspector was calm and composed. So far, there was no

harsh reaction. Then he looked at his postal order and picked it up and moved back towards the door, but did not go out. The Post Office was full of people waiting their turn. There were Italians who wanted to send money to their families in Italy and Somalis who wanted to send money to their families in the interior of the country. The hall was large and, besides money order counters, there was also a counter for people who wished to send telegrams. But, although the place was full of people and although I appeared to be getting on with my work, I was acutely conscious of the Inspector as he drew back from the crowd.

I lifted my eyes and looked across at him, because I was sure he was looking at me, and our eyes met. What would he do next?

The Inspector returned to the counter. He did not smile. He did not look around.

"Will my driving license be sufficient?" he asked.

"Yes," my colleague said, and payment was made to him.

Later, when I closed the counter and was on my way to the cash office to hand over my takings for the morning, I was surprised to find the same Inspector waiting for me in the corridor.

"I'd like to have a word with you," he said. "I was wrong the other day and I apologize."

I was surprised, but glad that we had ended the matter this way. I expect he was a man full of ambition, hoping to be Commandant at some police station, where his subordinates would only say 'yes' to whatever he decreed. But I also think he was a man of courage. If you make a mistake and do not realize it, you are liable to make more. A clean beginning always helps to build a clean society.

As for my personal fortunes, I was eventually promoted to Controller, replacing the Italian who held the post before me. The appointment was next in seniority to that of the Cashier. Along with the Cashier I signed every money-related voucher issued by the Post Office.

CHAPTER III

The Constituent Assembly

While we were being trained by the Italians to run this part of our country after independence, the British Administration was punishing us by giving away to Ethiopia part of the territories it was administering. In 1955, whilst we were under UN Trusteeship, Britain gave away to Ethiopia the Haud and the Reserved Area. Earlier, in 1948, after the visit of the UN Commission to Somalia, it had ceded a part of the Ogaden to Ethiopia. It is still not clear whether these actions were to demonstrate Britain's displeasure at the Somali politicians who failed to nominate Britain to administer the territories.

It is perhaps not too far fetched to suppose that Britain, which had advocated a united Somaliland, should be greatly angered when Somalia requested that Italy, a defeated country, be nominated as the administering power. To emphasize the point further, how could a nomad, a shepherd who walks barefoot, slight the British Empire—an Empire stretched across oceans and the Empire on whose territories the sun would never set.

I left my job at the Post Office and began working at the Constituent Assembly, where the Constitution of the new Republic was to be prepared. Apart from the Somali politicians, representatives from foreign countries were also involved in this endeavour.

I worked at the Record Office (*Ufficio Verbale*) of the Constituent Assembly. The Chief of the office was an Italian who taught us shorthand and typing. We were the only people in the Trust Territory learning shorthand and there were six of us. We had to be prepared to service the newly constituted Chamber of Deputies.

The National Assembly building was a large red brick building on the western side of the town centre. It had been built by the Italians during the Fascist period, and was known as *Casa del Fascio*.

National Assembly building.

The Assembly Hall itself was splendid. All the seating and fittings were of a high quality. The wall behind the President's bench was covered with a large painting by an Italian artist by the name of Novarese, and showed the masses—men, women and children—breaking the chains of colonialism. The Hall had a gallery where the public could sit and listen to debates. There were committee rooms off to the side, which members could use for additional business.

Our job was to record *verbatim* the proceedings of the Assembly. The speakers made their statements either in Somali, Arabic or Italian. The minutes were recorded in Italian, through a Somali interpreter. Some of the Deputies had no frame of reference to help them understand the new institution in which they found themselves. For the civil servants and army officers there was at least some kind of training and preparation for the tasks they were required to perform. Not so for the members of parliament, who were to sit in this Hall and make laws for the country. Many of them had come to the role straight from the interior representing rural constituencies.

As Muslims, most Somalis learnt to read the Koran in childhood. Some of the Deputies knew it by heart, and in their debates would frequently quote its verses. These were religious people rather than politicians and, if they could, they would have preferred to adopt the Holy Book as the Constitution of the country rather than the one now being prepared with the help of those they considered infidels.

For some members, the Hall itself seemed suffocating. Not because it was not well ventilated, but because they were accustomed to the open air, to doing business, negotiating inter-tribal issues and solving problems, in accordance with the Holy Book or tribal customs, sitting under a tree.

In the decade of preparation for independence, an attitude developed in which, if one was not able to speak good Italian he was considered rather primitive. So it was in the Assembly. Those who had been to Italy for their higher education would flaunt their knowledge, interrupting the interpreters and making their statements directly in Italian. Others who had learnt elementary Italian would start their speeches with 'Signor Presidente' and then revert to the Somali language.

Still others who were literate neither in Italian nor in Arabic, and who knew some Arabic words of greeting, not to be outdone, would start their speeches with the Arabic *Sayid ar-Raiis*.

The task before the Constituent Assembly was to prepare a draft Constitution, after which the Assembly was to be converted into a Legislative Assembly.

The person appointed Minister for the Constitution was the very same person who had once refused to obey the orders of the Prime Minister which, you may recall, required him to affix his thumbprint as an identification mark in connection with encashment of a postal order.

When the United Nations Four-Power Commission, made up of the United States of America, the Soviet Union, Britain and France, had visited Somalia in 1948, to ascertain the wishes of the inhabitants, the most influential of the Somali political parties, the SYL, had told the Commission unequivocally that they wanted Four-Powers joint rule for the country.

The United Nations General Assembly, by a Resolution on 21 November 1949, designated the area of ex-Italian Somaliland a UN Trust territory. But, instead of appointing the US, the USSR, Britain and France to oversee the transition to independence, it appointed three minor UN member States, namely the Philippines, Egypt and Colombia as its Advisory Council.

What could these three developing countries do, one wondered, for another similar, that itself had no source of income, even to maintain the few buildings that had been left behind by the Fascists? On the subject of the buildings, the two most solidly constructed edifices which we inherited, and which would clearly last long but which served no utilitarian purpose whatsoever for the country, were the Arch of Umberto di Savoia erected at the centre of the Mogadishu Garden, and the large Catholic Cathedral which dominated downtown Mogadishu. In addition to these there was the Parliament building already mentioned, and the *Governo* building which accommodated all departments of the Government.

In the Constituent Assembly, the Members' debate focused on establishing hierarchies of officers and leaders. No one seemed to be worried about how or from where the salaries of such officers would come. Every remuneration and 'perk' currently enjoyed by these leaders was paid out of the Republic of Italy's annual budget. According to the Trusteeship Council Official Records, (Twenty-second session, 9 June-1 August 1958):*

'Actual estimated receipts under the Italian Trusteeship Administration budget consist almost entirely of the Italian State grant of 54.2 million somalos. The principal items of estimated ordinary expenditure are 16.8 million somalos for personnel, 9 million somalos for military and police personnel and 4.7 million somalos for the air force. Extraordinary expenditure includes 8.7 million somalos to balance the Territorial budget and 10 million somalos for economic development.' Agriculture and livestock, the two main items that Somalia could develop, were not given much attention. Nor was the question of infrastructure. The harbour at Mogadishu was very inadequate; cargo and passenger ships had to anchor far out from the port, and goods and people were brought to shore by lighter. Yet, no provision was made to improve such facilities. Mogadishu was the capital city of a country which was going to be an independent republic at the end of the decade.

Though there did not appear to be any coordination with AFIS, the British Administration was in its own way also preparing British Somaliland for independence. But only the British Somaliland Protectorate was to be free. Nothing was being said about the NFD (the Northern Frontier District), a territory which was almost wholly inhabited by Somalis but which the United Kingdom was retaining control of together with its Kenya colony. The Ogaden was already in the mouth of the Lion of Judah, Haile Selassie of Ethiopia.

Once more the words from Bevin's speech in defence of a Greater Somaliland are a nagging reminder of what might have been:

'...In the latter part of the last century the Horn of Africa was divided between Great Britain, France and Italy. At about the time we occupied our part, the Ethiopians occupied an island

---

*   *Somaliland under Italian Administration;* p.15 para.109, UN New York 1958,

area which is grazing ground for nearly half of the nomads of British Somaliland for six months of the year. Similarly, the nomads of Italian Somaliland must cross the existing frontiers in search of grass. In all innocence, therefore, we proposed that British Somaliland, Italian Somaliland and the adjacent part of Ethiopia, if Ethiopia agreed, should be lumped together as a trust territory, so that the nomads should lead their frugal existence with the least possible hinderance and there might be a real chance of a decent economic life, as understood in that territory.'

In spite of this inspired thinking, the Somali nation had been made disjointed, and for the moment only two parts were becoming free, and under separate tutelage. And yet this was the only place in Africa where there was such homogeneity—all had the same religion, spoke the same language, practiced the same traditions, held in regard the same values, and enjoyed a common cultural heritage. A problem about to confront us was how the parts were to communicate with each other in government and administration. One part of us used Italian and the other English. Our own language, Somali did not have a script, and those who did not know one of the two colonial languages were considered illiterate, although Arabic was also widely spoken in the country.

It would, of course, have been difficult in 1948 for SYL politicians to have stated that they wanted such and such colonial power to rule. It was a more defensible and respectable position—if not a scape goat—to opt for the United Nations as an appropriate authority. But these politicians openly objected to the return of *Italian* rule. Britain was the power that put forward the Bevin Plan which the SYL leader referred to when he met the UN Commission in 1948 : '...When we saw [in the newspapers] this being uttered by a Foreign Minister of a Great Power we were very happy indeed because it is one of our great aims'.

If what Britain wanted to do was 'one of the our great aims', then why did the SYL not accept the British to administer the territories, especially if in the end they accepted Italy to take over. In the light of what was allowed to happen to the Somali territories, however, I am reminded of the Somali proverb which says: *Muraadkaaga maqaar ey ayaa loogu seexdaa*; "For your interests' sake you can even sleep on a dog's pelt.".

Denied the opportunity to administer the Somalilands under UN auspices, the British went their own way. The Somali parts under their control were not the concern of the United Nations, and they were not subject to UN Trusteeship rules. They did not need external approval of their plans for training the indigenous population. The offices in the Protectorate were manned by Indians, not Somalis. Even the typists were Indians. The currency of this part of the Somali territory until the Second World War was the Indian rupee and after that the East African shilling. The Courts were governed by the Indian Penal Code. Hindi words have come into our language through this association, words like *Bara Sahib* for governor, *dhobi* for laundry, *roti* for bread, *langare* for a lame person, and many more.

Independence Day for the United Nations Trusteeship Territory of Somalia was fixed for the 1st of July, 1960. Britain, however, decided to declare Independence Day for British Somaliland on 26th June 1960—four days before the former Italian Somaliland. Was this decision significant? Could it be remotely possible that by pre-empting the independence celebrations of the south by 4 days, Britain was demonstrating a still-felt displeasure at not having been given sole governance of the Somali territories.

The process of Independence was being worked out by limited groups in authority. The general public knew very little of what was taking place. For them, hardly anything was different. I am not sure that the people of the interior even knew that they would soon be masters of their own affairs. In Mogadishu itself, where everything was happening, I know for a fact that some inhabitants of Hamar Weyn were still in possession of Italian Lire, which had not been legal currency for over a decade. It is possible there were people who remained oblivious of the intervening years of British Military Administration and believed that the fascists were still in occupation. Italians from pre-Republican days had remained behind. They took up business activities and farming with impunity, they owned cinema houses in the capital, and operated their exclusive social clubs. Fascist symbols remained engraved on Mogadishu's walls when they should have been considered an offence—fascist hatchets engraved on the pillars of the defensive walls along the sea coast, paintings of Mussolini's head, and his helmet engraved on the walls of certain government buildings. All these remained untouched.

Preparations were almost complete for the celebrations of Independence Day. The people of both the north and the south were keen to have the two parts united, and agreement was reached among the politicians, that, together they would form just one republic—not a "Federal" republic or "United" republic—but the Republic of Somalia.

Ours was a country with no economic prospects. The Italians had encouraged the cultivation of banana for export to Italy at subsidized prices. Nothing had been done to develop the export potential of the pink or white varieties of grapefruit, the papayas, guavas, or the wide variety of other tropical fruits in which the country abounded. Apart from a small sardine cannery in Kandala there was no infrastructure to utilize the country's marine resources along 3,200 kilometres of coastline. The same was true of the livestock sector where, apart from a small beef cannery in Mogadishu, no development was planned. As far as any agro-industry is concerned the country possessed only a single 2,500 hectare sugar plantation and a sugar mill in Jowhar (*Villagio Duca degli Abbruzzi*), with an output of 88,909 quintals in 1956. *

Livestock, fishing and agriculture were three major potential sources of revenue. But in their present state, they certainly could not generate enough foreign exchange to balance the country's essential requirements from abroad. We needed to import everything from outside, ranging from needles to tractors. We did not have any large scale economic assets to manage, and as for our small scale economy, it was controlled by non-Somalis. What then did political independence mean if the country had to depend economically on foreign powers? During British colonial rule in India, there existed a situation similar to ours, whereby the colonial administration wished to prolong the process of handover by doing thing in small doses. The British attitude

* IBID p.17 para.123

there was that 'a people must fit itself for self-government by trying doses of gradually increasing strength.' The British proposed that the Indians first get to grips with running municipal and local bodies, and then the provincial government, but with 'safeguards'. This, they assured the Indians, would be followed by complete self-governance at the provincial level, which would in turn be followed by self-rule at the central government level. Mahatma Gandhi declined to accept this view. He believed the people's ability could be tested not by operating local administrations under British tutelage, but by undertaking large-scale economic and social reforms under their own leadership.*

As Somalia was an oral society. This emerging new Republic was going to be a country confused by foreign cultures, since, without a script for its language, its own culture could not impose itself in certain areas of life. All business, when not transacted orally, was dependent on how much one knew of one of the two foreign languages—English or Italian.

Similar economic and educational problems existed in British Somaliland. After completing intermediate education—the highest available in the Protectorate until 1955—only a few students, for whatever reason—accident or good fortune—went abroad for secondary studies to the Sudan. I have heard it said that Britain at one time planned to establish a College or a University at Daimole, near Sheikh town, but that the elders refused to have any such institution, believing it would bring with it the Christian religion. Such strongly held feelings, if true, may have been based on earlier stories which told of how, in 1901-4, the British attempted to convert to Christianity some orphans who had been collected from around the environs of Berbera town and housed in the Mission camp in Daimole village. For their part, the British would also not have forgotten the fierce 20-year Holy War waged against them in the early 20th century by Mohamed Abdille Hassan, whom the British dubbed 'The Mad Mullah of Somaliland'. Education and its interface

---

* *Gandhi's Technique of Mass Mobilization,* M.M. Verma; New Delhi 1990.

with religion had always been a sensitive issue among our people.

In most African countries, Christian missionaries addressed themselves to such individuals as were in need of shelter or food, or to those whom they considered animists. But in Somaliland, the people were not short of food, and belief in their religion was so strong that they avoided even going close to a European. They would more likely run away from him if he happened to pass by them, or would taunt him, shouting 'Gaal! Gaal!', meaning infidel.

Throughout their long stay in the country, the colonial powers were singularly unsuccessful in converting Somalis to Christianity, with the exception of very few families whom they had taken out of the country, and a handful of abandoned children who had unknown Italian fathers. This was one of the few countries in Africa where the missionaries totally failed in their vocation.

I remember how, in our schools the Italians taught us Italian history and geography, but the religion they taught us was Islam. I remember reading about the life of the Prophet Mohammed (pbuh) in Italian. The Italian Administration went so far as to bring Arabic teachers from Libya to teach Arabic and religion. The British, too, knew that education and religion were delicate areas. Even so, there were pioneering Somali teachers like Moallim Jama in Italian Somaliland and Mohamud Ahmed Ali in British Somaliland, who were strong advocates of education, and whose contributions to education are of historic significance.

Because the Somali elders on the whole felt that education posed a threat to the religion, they thought it their duty to guard the younger generation against what they saw as evil. They did not consider that we needed education to be able to run the country, that education was the key to our future progress. They were unconvinced that university students could be mature enough to defend themselves against conversion to Christianity.

Nevertheless,Somalis were sent to Italy to become graduates in political science, economics, law and other subjects. However, we were latecomers to education in comparison with certain other parts of Africa. Those who were taking on the mantle of leadership in the newly independent countries of Africa in the

1950s and 60s were generally much more educated than our Somali leadership, many having already pursued successful careers as teachers and university professors in the West, and as doctors, before coming to power.

In 1957, after about seven years of Italian Trusteeship Administration, we had, for example, only *two men* (Author's italics) under training in the diplomatic field. This was revealed by the Acting Administrator, Dr. Piero Franca, when he informed the U.N. Mission which visited the territory from 18 July to 6 August 1957 that '*an increasing number of Somali civil servants were receiving training in the diplomatic field—a Somali official had been appointed assistant to the Chef de Cabinet and another was serving in the Italian Embassy in Cairo.*'*

The Mission was also informed that 160 students were enrolled in the Higher Institute of Law and Economics (the only institution of higher education in the Territory) for the 1957-58 school year' and that thirty-seven Somalis were pursuing university studies in Italy.**

In 1960, the year of our independence, it was only expected that twentyseven Somalis would receive university degrees in Italy: 'one in medicine, six in political science, one in social science, nine in economics and business administration, one in journalism, three in veterinary medicine, two in agronomy, one in natural science, one in pharmacy and one in linguistics'.***

The celebrations for the independence of former Italian Somaliland and its union with British Somaliland, were to be held in the building of the Constituent Assembly—the parliament building. The edifice was to be fully illuminated for the occasion, which was to be so historic for the nation. Above the tower of the red-brick building, the Somalia national flag—sky blue with a five-pointed white star in the middle—was to be hoisted at midnight of 30 June/1 July 1960. That moment would denote the birth of the new Republic.

---

*   Trusteeship Council, Twenty-second Session—9 June-1
     August 1958—Supplement No. 2.
**   p.3 para.16
*** IBID p.26 para 200

Mogadishu was to be the capital of the Somali Republic. This was where the famous Moroccan traveller Ibn Batuta visited in 1331, and remarked that it was the capital of a prosperous Sultanate exporting skins and coloured cottons besides a number of exotic goods and ruled by a Sultan of Somali origin.

The Journal of African History, published in London in 1960, reveals that in the 13th century, Mogadishu had a currency of its own. A collection of 7,635 coins of twenty three rulers who are as yet unknown to numismatists and historians, suggests that Mogadishu minted its own coinage from 1300 to 1700.

The history of Somalia stretches back into the mists of time. Known as the "Land of Punt" in Pharaonic history, it had a close commercial relationship with the Egyptians, which touched its apex in the period of Queen Hatshep-Sut (about 1500 BC). To the Phoenicians, Somalia was also known as 'The Region of Incense'. All this was before the colonialists set foot on its territory. Somalia's viability and integrity lasted until the period of modern colonialism. The potential was still there. But neither the Italians nor the British wished to train the Somalis to raise the level of production so that the country could have a base for its economic development.

We Somalis were not at all worried about the economic aspect of independence. We were only anxious to get hold of the reins of power, taking everything else for granted. The truth, of course, was that whoever had control of the country's economy also held the power. If the new country was going to remain dependent economically on an ex-colonial power, the latter's continuous stay was guaranteed.

The first National Assembly was composed of members from only two of the five Somali territories. The British had already given piecemeal to Ethiopia huge tracts of land—the Ogaden and the Haud and the Reserved Area—and remaining under British control was the Northern Frontier District (NFD).

The National Assembly was composed of 123 members: 90 elected from the former Italian Somaliland and 33 from the former British Protectorate. We had no idea what the future held in store for us, although independence was something that everybody was expecting to enjoy. Those who had been elected or selected to take care of the welfare of the country were supposed to be the most responsible among us.

I recall that one of the members of the new National Assembly was a gentleman who had come almost every day, after the afternoon prayers, to my father's shop at Afar Irdood in Mogadishu's commercial area, to talk over a cup of tea. He was fairly advanced in age. I am certain he had never been to any modern school to learn either Italian or Arabic. He must have had some literacy in one language or another, or he would not have been allowed to become a candidate for the Assembly. In order to be eligible for election it was a prerequisite that one should know how to read and write. In fact, as I was to discover during the time I worked at the National Assembly secretariat, the literacy requirement had only been loosely enforced. Some of the Deputies would come to us in our office on the first floor and ask us to teach them how to write their signatures. It was important that they learn how to sign the attendance register to be included on the payroll. When Parliament was in session, it met each morning and afternoon. Before each sitting, the MPs present had to sign the attendance register which was placed on the left side of the chamber. The roll call of members present was then read out by the secretariat staff, and each member would respond loudly as his name was called. One would say '*Presente*', another would say 'Present', yet others would say '*Haadir*' or '*Waajooga*'—Italian, English, Arabic, Somali—it was like the Tower of Babel.

For those of us who were *reer magaala*, townspeople born and bred, and who had some (even if only a little) education, and considered ourselves sophisticated in our habits, there were other things which amused us as well. Worthy though they may have been to represent their constituents, some Deputies had hardly ever spent time away from their villages and may never have even seen the capital before. For some it was their first time wearing trousers, and it was obvious they were not very comfortable in them. Styles of dress also varied, from three-piece suits, to Egyptian style *khamis* or long shirts, to shirt and *macaawis* or sarong-type skirt, to various combinations of these—*khamis* and *macaawis, macaawis* and jacket, *khamis* and jacket. With all forms of dress, it became fashionable to wear the white embroidered fez-shaped hat for which the coastal town of Brava is famous. The President of the National Assembly, Aden Abdulle Osman, always wore the *koofi Barawe* , and the Brava hat became almost the symbol of an MP. The walking stick was another popular accessory.

Being in Parliament, there were some who became famous within a very short span of years. Of course, one of the duties of AFIS was precisely to create a core group of capable and prominent people so that the country could be handed over to them. To be famous, however, did not always mean to be capable.

There were some members who never took part in debates, but only in voting, and who were not averse to accepting incentives and inducements to vote a particular way. Generally, the voting pattern was decided even before members entered the Chamber.

An MP's salary was 600 Somali shillings a month in the early sixties. Later in 1969 this was raised to 2,000 shillings. The fee for attendance, *gettone di presenza,* was 20 shillings per session. (In the early sixties US$ 1.00 = Sh.6.30, and against the £ it was shilling for shilling. Today US$ 1.00 = Sh.6000-7000)

The Secretary-General of the National Assembly knew about my previous job at the Post Office. One day he asked me if I could handle accounts, as he needed somebody to fill in while the regular accountant was on leave. An Italian lady was in charge of the accounts. She prepared the pay-rolls each month for members of the Assembly as well as for the staff. Though there were many Somalis in the department, apparently no one else knew the job. So, for two months I occupied the neat, clean and well equipped office while she was on vacation in Italy with her husband.

It surprised me that the person who was supposed to be her assistant, and who showed me where everything was kept in the office had not been trained in the work. He uncovered a machine and asked if I knew how to use it. It was an electric calculator, of the type I had used at the Post Office.

It was inefficient not to have made contingency plans for salaries and allowances to be paid, especially salaries and allowances of such important and vocal people as parliamentarians and those foreigners who serviced our young Republic's institutions. Perhaps it was not the Italian woman's fault but her boss who was to blame. Perhaps it was he who had not wanted his subordinates to learn too much about how things were done. It was not unusual for officers not to want to share information with their staff, especially when money was involved. The Secretary-General was not in any case a very trusting man, and I knew he did not like me. But on this occasion he had needed somebody with my skill to do a job. He would not remain in office very long himself if he failed to pay the salaries and allowances of the parliamentarians and ex-patriate staff of the Secretariat.

In my regular job as a stenographer at the Parliament, I and the other members of the pool, we were required to record verbatim and in Italian all the parliamentary debates, which were then translated by Drs Morcos and Skook into Arabic and English. All the business of the Parliament had to be documented in Italian, English and Arabic, the three working languages of the parliament. The system was very cumbersome. But that was not the entire problem. As many of the members were not sufficiently fluent in any one of the languages to be able to refer to the records themselves, they needed someone to provide oral translations of the documents to them in the Somali language.

Although it was hard work, I felt privileged to be a part of the system. It was always interesting. It was the house from which all the laws emanated. It was here that the first President of the Republic would be elected. It was here one met the political personalities of today and others who were destined to feature prominently in the future politics of our nation.

The President of the National Assembly, later to become the first President of the Republic, was Aden Abdulle Osman, a highly respected gentleman. With his grey hair and perfect sense of dress, he always looked the statesman. When he sat in his elevated position at the front of the chamber, the whole House was like a classroom, the members looking like school children in the presence of a firm teacher. I remember once, a member was at the microphone, below the President's chair, and the President obviously felt he was talking irrelevantly. When the MP ignored his request to stop, the President took his own microphone and brought it down on the member's head. "*Aamus!*" he said.

The President used spectacles for reading. Whenever he disapproved of a member's attitude, he would just raise his spectacles and look at the person. Without saying a word, it was clear that he meant him to shut up.

I enjoyed listening to what the Deputies had to say in the Chamber, especially the out-of-town Deputies who talked about the problems of their villages. They would, for example, appeal to the Government to dig wells in their areas, and of course they were right. The irony of the situation was that even the capital had no potable water. Drinking water was brought to most households in Mogadishu in used petrol canisters on the backs of donkeys.

Time passed and the date for the independence of Italian Somaliland and union with the former British Somaliland drew near. In readiness for this new chapter, we could offer a few bureaucrats, but we had no medical doctors, engineers, agronomists or geologists of our own. Illiteracy in the country was very high. For the election of Deputies to the National Assembly it was necessary for the various competing parties to be represented on ballot papers by picture symbols and not words. As a people, Somalis are generally highly politicized, and although most of the voters knew whom they wished to elect, it remained uncertain that their vote went for their chosen candidate.

There were plenty of stories of how votes were manipulated, how, in some instances, voters were told to put a cross on an insignia to denote their party preference, and in other instances to put a cross on the same insignia to indicate the opposite! True or untrue, Somalis are skilled raconteurs, and we entertain each other with humourous interpretations and jokes about even the gravest of our national events.

The stage was set. There was independence for two Somali territories. There was euphoria over our future prospects. We did not have a very extensive infrastructure, but neither was our population very large, only about 3 million. And we had vast rangelands populated by our nomad families and their herds of camel, sheep and goats, and cattle; small urban communities populated the district towns and market centres which dotted the map. We were a people who learnt quickly, we were proud, and the future was ours. It was a time of great hope and expectations. A nation of republicans, we had been called, and every one his own sultan.

CHAPTER IV

The Historic Day

People started gathering in Parliament Square from the afternoon of 30 June 1960. While waiting for the hour of freedom at midnight they chanted and danced. The Parliament building where I worked had been strung with coloured lights, as had the streets of the city. We spent the whole day working and none of us went home for lunch. In fact, we stayed at work until the next morning. At sundown the lights went on, the city's main streets were shining brightly and the people were in festive mood. My colleagues and I were strategically placed on the roof of the building from where we could see the Square below us. Most importantly, we were very close to the flag pole where the Somali national flag was to be hoisted.

The Italian Administrator, in the presence of the United Nations Advisory Council Members, was to hand over the administration of the country to its elected leaders. Our flag was to be hoisted to the accompaniment of the National Anthem of the new Republic and would be given a 21 gun salute. The National anthem's title was *Soomaaliya Ha Noolaato* Long Live Somalia. It had only a title and no words. Again, it had been composed by an Italian.

Loud-speakers, installed at the four corners of the Parliament building, were blaring out the programme of events to the crowds. At a certain moment, the announcer requested the crowds to be silent, and that started the count-down to midnight. Everyone was looking at their watches; no one wanted to miss the historic moment when the Republic was born. The crowd's eyes were rivetted on the flag pole which was floodlit from all sides.

The conductor of the band called his musicians to attention, he raised his baton in readiness, waiting for the signal to go. Midnight: the first moments of the 1st of July 1960, and the Somali flag was raised. The Republic of Somalia was born. The crowd exploded in joy, and drums beat and the whole Square, overflowing with people, was in motion as figures jumped up and down, shouting "Long Live Somalia!" "*Soomaaliya Ha Noolaato! Soomaaliya Ha Noolaato.*"

We hugged each other. We laughed. We wept tears of happiness. We prayed for the country saying, "May Allah make it great." We danced. Women ululated. We congratulated each other. And this went on throughout the night, till the next morning.

One notable personality involved in the process of leading our part of the country to freedom, but who finally missed the celebrations was Kamal Eddin Salah, the Egyptian member of the United Nations Advisory Council, who had been assassinated in Mogadishu in 1957. Many people knew why Kamal Eddin Salah was in Somalia, but very few knew why now he was no more there.

On the first day of our independence, at its first session, the National Assembly approved the nation's first Constitution, and elected Aden Abdulle Osman as the First President of the Republic.

The President immediately moved to the official Presidential residence, *Villa Somalia,* formerly known as *Villa Italia.* The compound actually contained three villas, one which was the residence, one the offices, and the third the official Guest House. They were small villas, each consisting of four or five rooms and a small sitting room. The gardens were large, and planted with flame trees, bougainvillaea, hibiscus and varieties of other tropical trees and shrubs typical of the region. In comparison to the extensive grounds, the buildings, especially the residence and the offices, were modest for a Head of State.

The National Flag, hoisted on 1 July 1960, had a special significance for the Somali nation. Sky blue with a white star at the centre, the five points of the star were representative of the five Somali territories of Italian Somaliland, British Somaliland, the French Somali Coast (Djibouti), the Northern Frontier District (N.F.D.), and the Ogaden.

The new Republic had so far achieved the union of only the first two points of the star. With regard to the remaining Somali

Aden Abdulle Osman
First President
of the Republic, 1960-67.

Abdirashid Ali Shermarke:
Prime Minister 1960-64,
and President 1967-69.

Abdirazak Haji Hussein:
Prime Minister 1964-67.

Mohamed Haji Ibrahim Egal:
Prime Minister 1967-69.

territories still under alien rule the Constitution stated in AR-
TICLE 6, Paragraph 4:

> The Somali Republic shall promote, by legal and peaceful means,
> the union of Somali territories and encourage solidarity among
> the peoples of the world, and in particular, among African and Is-
> lamic peoples.'

That we had been unable to move further along this road already, and had not taken advantage of the one-time powerful international support for this position, has to be judged as political
shortsightedness, and as a massive historic failure on the part of
our politicians.

Britain was unlikely ever again to support unification of the
Somali territories. The Lion of Judah, the so-called 'King of
Kings' would never give up the Somali territories under his control through legal and peaceful means. We had only to look at the
evidence. During a visit to the Ogaden on 25 August 1956, Haile
Selassie warned the people: 'We remind you, finally, that all of
you are by race, colour, blood and custom, members of the great
Ethiopian family. Although, there may be local dialects, we must
always strive to preserve our unity and our freedom.' Speaking
about the unity of all the Somali territories, he had said : 'As to
the rumours of a greater Somalia, we consider that all the
Somali peoples are economically linked with all Ethiopia, and,
therefore, we do not believe that such a state can be viable standing alone, separated from Ethiopia.'*

The new Republic would have to deal with such a man. This
man, who called himself the oldest statesman in Africa had already annexed Eritrea, and did not have the title of Emperor for
nothing. Haile Selassie played ball with the colonial powers and
became the black-skinned, blue-eyed boy of the Western Powers.

As it happened, Ethiopia began harassing our young Republic
shortly after its independence, through border skirmishes.
Being newly independent, we had not even had time to establish
proper security along our borders; we were a soft target. Yet, the
Somalis have been standing firm against Abyssinian encroach-

*   Emperor Haile Selassie's Speech in the Ogaden, 25 August
    1956: Extract: *Ethiopian Observer,* December 1956.

ments from at least the 16th century, and something in our national character and in our inbred commitment to the lands we
inhabit has kept us strong against this neighbour throughout
our history.

The National Assembly elected Jama Abdullahi Ghalib as its
President on 7 July 1960. He was one of the members from
former British Somaliland. He spoke Arabic and English and, of
course, Somali. The already-established practices of the Record
Office of the Parliament continued. Since my Italian Chief, and
my colleagues and I took our notes in Italian, the President and
all other English- or non-Italian-speaking members, could not
know if their statements and interventions were being correctly
recorded or not. They had to wait till the English translations
were made available.

The whole business of the nation was being conducted
through the medium of a foreign language, which only few of us
had started learning just ten years earlier. The President of the
Republic and the Prime Minister were both Italian speaking, but
by no means were all the Deputies from ex-Italian Somalia
fluent in the language. Further, the Italian language was not an
international language that could be used in contacts with other
countries of the world. It seemed fit only for use in our offices and
for exchanging notes with the Italian Government. To cor-
respond with most other governments a knowledge of our other
colonial language, English, was necessary. There was obviously
a continuing role in the country for foreigners, not least for draft-
ing official correspondence.

The six of us who serviced the National Assembly had initially
been selected for the job from a field of one hundred young men
and women who were enrolled in the course for shor-
thand/typing. The man who had trained us was Signor Lucio
Valent, and we were now an elite corps—the only people who
could do the job. I loved the work, and I knew I was performing a
useful service for my country. But there were problems awaiting
me round the corner.

Four months after independence, an article appeared in an
Opposition party newspaper, criticizing the Secretary General of
the Assembly for retaining the services of his Italian accountant
when there was a Somali who could do the job. This was the

honeymoon period of independence when we enjoyed a free press.

The newspaper article insinuated that the Secretary General was involved in misuse of funds, and that he wished to retain the Italian woman because she was prepared to cover up for him. It was clear that the Somali being referred to in the article was myself, since I had filled in for the accountant whilst she was on vacation. The newspaper was published in Arabic, but the article would have had to be translated into Italian for the Secretary General, who spoke no Arabic, and for his Italian accountant to understand it.

It is worth reflecting that in those far away days we had the beginnings of a democratic system, and we enjoyed freedom of speech, freedom of press, and freedom of association. They were halcyon days.

The Secretary General was naturally furious about these public insinuations, as was the accountant. Neither of them spoke to me after the article appeared; they clearly thought I was behind it, even if I had not actually written the article. I expected some kind of vengeful action to be taken by the Secretary General, who in any case had never liked me. What happened, however, was totally unexpected. Apparently, the Secretary General had sent a copy of the article to the President of the Republic.

Within a few days President Aden Abdulle Osman called both of us to his office to discuss the matter. He had obviously been briefed by my boss and told me that I should not indulge in malicious behaviour towards my senior officers, should show respect for my Secretary General, that I had hurt the feelings of the Italian Signora and so on. It was clear that even the President thought I had written the article or at least knew something about it.

I was uncertain how I should behave towards a Head of State, and I was in awe at meeting him face to face. But, uppermost in my mind, even though I was only a simple stenographer and part-time accountant, I could not accept the responsibility for something I had not done.

A little later, while the three of us were walking side-by-side in the garden of Villa Somalia, the President spread his arms out over both our shoulders, like a good friend. This gesture gave me the courage I had been trying to summon.

"Mr. President," I said, "my feeling is that the Secretary General knows very well who the real author of that article is. I certainly do. But I think it was easier for him to blame it on me. It was true that the article seems to speak about me, but I did not write it and did not have anything to do with it."

In truth, of course, the article said nothing that the Secretary General could have sent a rejoinder to, and the newspaper had conveyed what was a very common and nationalistic view of the time, questioning why an Italian should be in a job that could be done by a Somali. After all, what had the ten years of training been for?

As people from the Northern part of the Republic began moving south to take up their places in the central government, new problems for the unified administration emerged, and the question of continued dependence on non-Somalis remained to be answered. Since officers from the northern part spoke and wrote English, they could not communicate with the Italian experts and not, in writing, with their Italian-educated Somali colleagues. Their offices were often supported by an English expert or an Indian clerk. It seemed that, whatever the official business to be transacted it had to be done through and was to be known to the foreign experts, some of whom were framing actual policy for our officials!

The Secretary General's animosity towards me increased following the newspaper incident, and the atmosphere at work became impossible to bear. It was clear I could not expect any promotion. I came to the conclusion that I must leave my job. In fact, I abandoned the job. To use a military term, I deserted, and left the country.

Along with forty others, I was offered a scholarship in the People's Republic of China. Although the new national government of independent Somalia had pro-Western leanings, it did not create any obstacle to prevent us from accepting the offer of scholarships from a communist country. During the early years, the Western governments offered scholarships to Somali students mainly through the Ministry of Education, while the Communist Bloc governments offered scholarships through the

Government, or to private individuals, as well as through political parties. Both the blocs were working hard to influence young African students so that they could spread their philosophies after returning home.

We left Mogadishu for Beijing by air, via Rome and Vienna to Prague, and then by train from Prague to Moscow, and from Moscow on the famous trans-Siberian railway route and through snow-covered Siberia to reach our destination in mid-November 1960. In Prague, the Chinese Embassy provided us with overcoats and other winter clothing for all of us, it was the first time we had ever left the country, and without these warm clothes we would certainly have frozen during our long journey through Siberia.

None of us knew anything about the customs and traditions or the contemporary situation of China. We knew that the Chinese were Asian, and something about their appearance, but that was all. We could only reassure each other by recalling what the Prophet Mohamed had once said:

"Go you even to China if you have to, in pursuit of education and knowledge" (*Hadith*). This was our inspiration.

When we arrived at the Beijing Railway Station we were welcomed by officials of the Chinese Ministry of Education and a Sudanese student. We soon found that, we were not the only foreign students. There were students from Albania, Chad, Ghana, Indonesia, Italy, Romania, the Soviet Union, Syria, Uganda, Vietnam, Yemen and Zanzibar. But we Somalis were one of the largest groups in those days.

All the foreign students, regardless of their different religious beliefs and national backgrounds, were housed in the same compound and had a common eating place. The school gave us coupons for food and for cotton material, the kind of cotton material that the whole Chinese population was dressed in during those days. Only the cotton material was bought with coupons, while the silk and woollen materials were sold off ration. A few months after we arrived we, the Somalis, submitted a petition to the Chinese authorities demanding:

1. A room in our building for offering our prayers;

2. A Muslim restaurant for the Somalis and any other Muslim students who wished to eat there; and

3. An increase in the scholarship allowance from Yuan 80,00.
(US$1 = 2.00 Chinese Yuan then)

The Chinese Authorities asked us to try and appreciate the difficult economic situation the country was facing. It was true. In the sixties, the situation in China was very hard, but we still thought that what we were asking was reasonable, and would not make any difference to their overall problems. They knew that if the Somali students were not satisfied and decided to return home, China's image would suffer and anti-communist forces in the world could make propaganda of the case. However, our demands had not been made to embarrass the Chinese authorities or to put them in a tight spot.

The first two demands were conceded to us, and eventually the third too, although it took some time.

In those years, the People's Republic of China faced shortages of both food and fuel. Buses were running with gas filled in huge rubber tanks on the top of the bus. Their problems increased further when the Soviet Union decided to stop its aid to China following the political differences between the two countries. A portrait of Mao Tse Tung and Nikita Krushchev was hung on the walls of all offices. After the break up of the 'brotherhood' the portraits had to be cut in half, and Krushchev removed.

In April 1961, the Chinese Authorities wanted us to organize a demonstration on the occasion of African Liberation Day, which in those years was celebrated on 15 April. This was before the foundation of the Organization of African Unity (OAU) (25 May 1963). They prepared all kinds of slogans attacking the imperialists and colonialists, and wrote them on big bill-boards.

When we Somalis were informed about the planned demonstration, we agreed to join it. We also prepared a board saying 'Down with Ethiopian Colonialism, Down with Haile Selassie.' and asked the Chinese to prepare its Chinese version. This was a big shock to them. They immediately convened a meeting of the African Students Association and told us that the Chinese authorities could not approve the Somali students' request, adding that the demonstration was for African Liberation Day and should not be used to attack another African country. It was clear that the Chinese meant us to attack only America and Japan. We argued that for Somalis, colonialists were colonialists, and colonialism had no colour. Only a short while earlier, Ethiopian forces had inflicted casualties on our people; and we Somali students were at the time wearing pieces of black cloth pinned to our chests as a sign of mourning for those who had been killed.

As there was a deadlock, we left the meeting. A few days later, the Authorities sent a gentleman to us, a black from the West Indies, whose name I do not now remember. We agreed to meet him and the Secretary-General of the African Students Association who was a Ghanaian, and student representatives from Chad and Uganda. But the subject was deadlocked again, with the West Indian and the student Secretary General defending the Chinese position, and the other two remaining silent. We refused to budge from our view that, if all colonialists, imperialists and their lackeys were not condemned, the Somalis would stay away from the demonstration. And, it happened that we stayed away.

Later, I discovered that the West Indian gentleman who had tried to mediate was in China as a political refugee. He had been given permanent residence by the Chinese in a hotel, and supplied with a car.

Apart from this particular conflict of interests which we experienced, the Chinese Authorities were always kind and courteous to their foreign guests, and despite all the difficulties they faced, they tried to make us feel as comfortable as possible.

The African students in China came from countries which were former colonies of the Western Powers. We had no previous experience of standing in queues for food or being issued ration tickets for our share of goods that were in short supply. But for me personally, it was a good lesson in many ways, including patience, and I was able to experience first-hand a very politically significant period of China's history.

There must have been many things about us foreign students which irritated the Chinese. One thing in particular that annoyed them was to see foreigners walking hand-in-hand with Chinese girls on the streets of Beijing. For them, this kind of behaviour was indecent while for most of the foreigners, particularly for Europeans and most Africans it was unremarkable. The Chinese Authorities were too discreet to interfere and advise us directly, but we had it on good authority that the offending girls were called to the appropriate office and lectured on their duty to uphold their country's honour and dignity.

Some time in 1961 we were told by the Chinese Authorities that Dr. Kwame Nkrumah, President of the Republic of Ghana was due to come to China on an official visit.

The news touched us deeply as this was the first time that we were meeting such a great son of Africa, President of Ghana, formerly the Gold Coast, which, at its independence in 1957 was one of the very few African countries to be free. Kwame Nkrumah was the man who really shook the colonialists with his stauch Pan-Africanist attitude, the man who said to the world, specially to Africa that Ghana's independence was meaningless if it was not linked to the total liberation of Africa.

We were told by the Chinese Authorities that the African students will go to the airport to welcome the African leader.

Among the Ghanaian students in Beijing at the time there were twin brothers whom we called the Tettehs and who were trumpet players. When they knew of the arrival of the Osagyefo they taught us a song dedicated to Pan-Africanism, which went like this:

There is victory for us
There is victory for us

In the struggle of Africa
There is victory for us

Sons of Africa arise
Sons of Africa arise

In the struggle of Africa
There is victory for us

Forward ever
Backward never

In the struggle of Africa
There is victory for us

The day of the arrival of that charismatic leader we were all in festive mood and lined up near the VIP lounge of Beijing International Airport. As soon as he alighted from the aircraft he was greeted with a 21-gun salute. Immediately after, he started shaking hands with the dignitaries and we the African students at once started singing, with really high spirit and enthusiasm, and to the accompaniment of the Tettehs' trumpets.

During his visit the Osagyefo, Dr. Kwame Nkrumah, also received us in his residence and talked to us about the future of our continent. We were so overwhelmed at being with such a great man who had such vision for Africa, and who, as we were to realise, was ahead of his time.

I returned home at the beginning of 1962. By then the Secretary General of the Somali National Assembly, my old boss, had been replaced. But I did not return to my former job. Only a day after my arrival home, I was offered a post at the Ministry of Information, and began working as parliamentary correspondent on the Government's Italian-language daily newspaper *Il Corriere della Somalia*.

At 'Il Corriere' most of the news was received directly from the Italian news agency, ANSA, via radio telegraph (RT). There was an Italian working on the paper who checked and corrected the despatches as they came in. The paper had only four pages. On the first page, we put the Government news of the day and major news from abroad. On the second page were the official communications and announcements. The third page contained letters and opinions of the public, and the fourth was for continuation of items from earlier pages. Every night, before the newspaper was closed, the Director of the Ministry of Information would visit the Printing House, which accommodated our office and the linotypes and printing machines, to see if everything was in line with government policy and that there were no news items that might annoy any friendly country. ANSA later provided some much needed technical assistance to the newspaper in the form of an experienced journalist, who at the same time worked as a correspondent for the Agency.

Like everything else in the early days of independence, it was a struggle to get things going correctly. With newspaper work, there is always pressure to meet deadlines, and we had our frequent crises and made frequent blunders, but we also had some laughs.

Customarily, when Somali students returned from Italy, after completing their education, they would come to the newspaper and ask us to publish their names, with photographs and biographical information. We usually tried to give them this bit of publicity, and no one was charged money for it.

One evening one such young man came to the office and as usual I directed him to the adjoining room where he could type up his piece. He did so and left, and I passed his work on to the Italian colleague for correction and editing.

"This is not Italian," he yelled.

"Well it should be," I yelled back. "He is an architect, graduated from Italy. If that is not Italian then you Italians haven't taught him properly."

He grew even more annoyed and said, "Maybe he was just a very bad student."

"And maybe he was a very good student in his field," I replied.

"It is just that building a grammatically correct sentence in Italian is so much harder than building a house!" and we both started laughing.

CHAPTER V

The Legacies We Inherited

The new Government led by Dr. Abdirashid Ali Shermarke faced great difficulties from the very beginning. The country had no economy to sustain itself let alone the ability to thwart Ethiopia's destabilizing plans. The mighty forces of the 'King of Kings', 'the Lion of Judah' had already threatened the young Republic.

Although our Constitution stated that we repudiated war as a means of settling international disputes, it was very clear that our dispute with Ethiopia could not be solved by peaceful means alone.

We were genuinely committed to securing the sovereign and independent rights of our people who remained under foreign powers. This was not a task that could be accomplished merely by pious wishes and slogans. Our problem was that we were not in a position to take any concrete action.

The Somali Republic was alone, without powerful patrons or allies. In international and regional forums, the two countries— Ethiopia and Somalia—were constantly being advised to settle their differences peacefully, which was tantamount to saying that we should accept the *status quo*.

When the Winds of Change swept through Africa in the sixties, most of the newly independent countries, being French or English-speaking had, through their common colonial ties, been encouraged to join together in regional or transcontinental groupings, with the idea of economic and political development. Not so Somalia. It was apparently not eligible to join any club not the Commonwealth Association, nor the East African Community, nor the *Organization Commune Afro-Malagasy* (O.C.A.M.) of French speaking Africa.

In 1962, the issue of the Somalis in the Northern Frontier District came into sharp focus. The Somalis in this area, still under British control, organized themselves politically and demanded to be allowed to join the independent Somali Republic. In October the same year the British Government appointed a Commission 'to ascertain and report on public opinion in the NFD.' Barely three months later, in December, the Commission reported that five of the six sub-districts of the Northern Frontier District favoured union with the Somali Republic. The Commission appointed by Britain to the NFD comprised Mr. G.C.M. Onyuke, Q.C. from Nigeria, Head of the Commission; and Maj.General M.P. Bogert, from Canada, Deputy Head.

Contrary to the Commission's findings, the British Government announced, in March 1963, that it was transferring the whole of the NFD to Kenya, which itself was scheduled to gain independence in December 1963.

Britain was again riding roughshod over the wishes of our people, and there was nothing we could do about it. We had no leverage with Britain, we did not have a powerful international ally to take up our cause, and we had no power ourselves, military or otherwise, with which to fight the case. In terms of a national security force, ours was the weakest in the region. (see table) Moreover, our colonial heritage left us isolated and at odds with both of our neighbours.

The combined military strength of Ethiopia and Kenya was 79,000, whereas Somalia's armed forces including its army, police and other security forces was 9,400 only. Why had Britain bothered to send a fact-finding mission to the NFD to ascertain public opinion, and then ignored the outcome? Angered and exasperated by the British move, Prime Minister Abdirashid Ali Shermarke tabled a motion in the National Assembly calling for breaking off diplomatic relations with Britain in protest against the British decision to give the NFD to Kenya. And, on 14 March 1963, Somalia severed diplomatic relations with Britain.

The question of why the British Government should have acted this way when it had itself sent the Commission to the NFD was puzzling then, and is still puzzling today. Since 1945, the principle of self-determination has been recognized as a legal concept, as enshrined in 'the principle of equal rights and self-determination of peoples' in Article 1(2), Article 55, and Articles 73, and 74 of the Charter of the United Nations.

The *Observer* newspaper of London commented at the time:

TABLE

THE STATE OF ARMED FORCES OF ETHIOPIA, KENYA AND THE SOMALI REPUBLIC IN 1965

COUNTRY	SIZE OF ARMED FORCES	POLICE AND OTHER SECURITY FORCES	SOURCES OF EXTERNAL MILITARY ASSISTANCE	DEFENCE AGREEMENT
ETHIOPIA	25,000 TO 35,000	30,000	United States, Sweden, Norway, India, Israel United Kingdom	With Kenya
KENYA	2,500	11,500	United Kingdom	With Ethiopia
SOMALI REP.	4,600	4,800	Italy, Soviet Union, United Arab Republic, United Kingdom	With none

Compiled from the following source: *Africa Report*, January 1964 pp.8-11-12 and 18 "The Armies of Africa" (Case Studies in African Diplomacy), Daresalam, Tanzania, 1969.

'By every criterion, the Kenya Somalis have a right to choosetheir own future. They differ from other Kenyans not just tribally but in almost every way....A better solution would be for Britain to refer the matter to the United Nations'.*

Besides the mainland Somalilands, Britain also had the island of Socotra under its control. According to Everyman's *Encyclopaedia,* Socotra is an 'island in the Indian Ocean, 250 km north-east of Cape Guardafui'. In fact, from Cape Guardafui on the Somali Horn, the closest mainland point, one can even see oil lamps burning on the island.

After leaving the former Italian Somaliland, Britain retained the island within its sphere of influence, and administered it with its Aden and South Yemen colony. Neither the Yemenis nor the Somalis showed any acute awareness of or interest in the island, and it appears that the Somalis probably lost it by default, and that the Yemenis, likewise, gained it by luck. If Britain had expected the 'difficult' Somalis to lay claim to the island and become involved in a territorial conflict with yet another neighbour, in this instance they must have been disappointed. Perhaps, the Republic had not even realized there were islands so near its own coast! In 1967 Socotra became part of a newly-independent South Yemen.

The Somali Republic inherited a backward and under-developed economy and a high percentage of illiteracy. Lack of educated and skilled personnel made us dependent on foreign expertise for the daily running of the administration and economic sectors. Somalia survived with assistance, just enough for sustenance. The aid was given by the former colonial powers, who were giving greater tranches of aid to our enemies. How could a Government begin to think of liberating a territory when it could not provide food and proper medical treatment to the people it was already responsible for? These were the practical issues. But the philosophical issues, and issues of principle were too great to ignore.

Three years after independence, a case came before the High

* *Case Studies in African Diplomacy, No II,*
  'Ethiopia-Somali-Kenya Dispute 1960-67'; OUP 1969

Court against a group of young army officers who were accused of attempting to overthrow the Government. They were from former British Somaliland. The case was heard by a British judge. The Government was represented by an Italian prosecutor, and the accused were defended by Indian lawyers who had been hired from Kenya. The law was the Indian Penal Code. Such was the state of affairs in the sovereign republic of Somalia in 1963: in the area of former British Somaliland the Courts used the Indian Penal Code, while in the area of former Italian Somaliland the Italian Penal Code was prevalent.

Although Somalia was considered a pro-Western country in the early sixties, the Prime Minister, Dr. Abdirashid Ali Shermarke, was becoming impatient with Western attitudes towards Somalia and Somali aspirations. In late 1963, the Somalia Government rejected an offer of more than US $10m in military assistance, extended jointly by the USA, West Germany and Italy, because it was considered inadequate and because of the political conditions attached to it. Instead, the Somali Government decided to accept a substantially larger Soviet military aid offer; according to unofficial sources this was reported to be about US $30 million.*

The ruling elite must have been totally naive not to realize that the Western Powers would never tolerate any geo-strategic development that might harm Ethiopia or Kenya, with whom it had strategic agreements. Moreover, in our part of the world, religion played an important role in politics and the Western Powers were more sympathetic to our adversaries, with whom they shared religion. But according to Saadia Touval's *Somali Nationalism,* 'traditionally, from Tsarist times, the Russians had felt particular sympathy for Ethiopia. In the late nineteenth century there was considerable discussion in Russia about the supposed affinity between the Orthodox Church and Ethiopian Christianity. Furthermore, the first hospital in Addis Ababa was established by the Russian Red Cross. After the Second World War, the interest in Ethiopia was reaffirmed with the dispatch of a Soviet medical team to staff a new hospital.'

*   IBID pp. 46-7.

Perhaps Dr. Abdirashid was influenced by the politics of the Egyptian leader, Gamal Abdel Nasser, who was a friend and ally of Somalia, and who had provided substantial aid to the country relative to its own resources. Nasser had turned to the Soviet Union for assistance for the construction of the Aswan Dam, after suffering disappointment at the negative attitude of Western governments to his national development programme.

Notwithstanding the Government tilt towards the Soviet Union, the country's domestic policy remained unchanged. Speech was free, and several independent newspapers, owned and published by different political parties, pressure groups, and young intellectuals continued to openly criticise the Government. Among the prominent journals appearing at the time in Mogadishu were *Dalka* and *La Tribuna,* which openly criticized the Government. There were protests, strikes and demonstrations galore against the Government, and trade unionism had a voice.

In the first years of independence, the issue of the introduction of a script for the Somali language would periodically be brought up. At one stage, when rumours spread that the Government intended to adopt the Latin script, there was a huge demonstration after the Friday prayers, with the crowd chanting the slogan: "Latin, Ladin", the latter word is Arabic for atheism or without religion. Some of the people saw the advocacy of the Latin script for Somali over the Arabic script as an unwelcome involvement of a foreign hand. The religious pressure groups were powerful and, for the moment the Government had to postpone taking the decision.

Later in 1964, when Abdirazak Haji Hussein became the Prime Minister, replacing Shermarke, he too met with little success in dealing with the problem of the colonized territories. Instead, he turned his energies to the unenviable task of national administrative reforms. The reorganization was to be based, he said, on the principle of *'l'uomo giusto al posto giusto',* 'the right man for the right job'. The result was more than a little chaotic. He began sacking high-ranking officials from their jobs on what appeared to be a whim rather than a well-defined set of criteria

This phase came to be known as the period of the dreaded *busta rossa,* from the Italian words meaning 'red envelope'. It was usual for Government offices to use red envelopes (actually, more orange than red in colour) for their mail, and Abdirazak's letters of dismissal to officials whom he considered incompetent arrived in such envelopes. What had till then been the harmless standard government envelope acquired the new connotation of a 'letter bomb'. In most cases, of course, the envelopes contained quite innocuous information or even offer of promotion, but recipients would be stunned at the first sight of the envelope, expecting the worst. *Busta rossa* was on everybody's lips, and mention of it today may still brings a wry smile to the faces of those who remember the period.

Although the government of Abdirazak became notorious as 'the Government of the Red Envelopes', on the plus side, he instituted a system of financial rewards as incentives to officials who were hard-working and productive, and the pay structure of the civil service was, for the first time and the only time in our history, revised with some merit.

On 10 June 1967, in the Presidential elections, the ex-Prime Minister, Dr. Abdirashid Ali Shermarke, replaced Aden Abdulle Osman as President. A month later, 15 July 1967 he appointed Mohamed Haji Ibrahim Egal, a prominent politician from the former British part of the territory, as the Prime Minister. Egal had actually been the Head of Government of an independent northern Somaliland in June 1960 for the four days before the independence of the south and the union of the two parts.

The President had changed, and so had the Prime Minister, but the country's economic situation remained the same. The country did not generate enough revenue to even cover the salaries of its civil servants. We were dependent on budgetary support from the developed countries, mostly Italy. The main employer in the country was the Government and those who were employed by it had to maintain many others of the extended family who remained unemployed. By the mid-sixties the influx from the rural areas to the capital had increased phenomenally. Most of the people from the interior who migrated to the capital were illiterate, unskilled and unemployable in the urban economy. They roamed about aimlessly on the streets or sat in tea-houses gossiping and sipping tea at the expense of their relatives employed in various offices of the government.

Many migrants to the capital came to seek monetary favours from the parliamentarians whom they had helped to get elected to the National Assembly. And indeed, the ministers and influential deputies did dole out funds to people from their constituencies when they came to the city. Both the Prime Minister and the Minister for Internal Affairs were overseers of special budgets (*fondo politico*) for constituency business. These funds were unaccounted for in the national budget and were, as it was commonly believed paid out as political patronage to individuals rather than utilized for the direct benefit of communities. A number of individual fortunes were purportedly made through such handouts and bribes.

Corruption, nepotism, and tribalism were alive and prospering. They were the roads to success. This was a period when the criterion for getting a job or a promotion was *not what you know, but who you know.*

Neither were the governments of foreign nations bothered about the proper utilization of their aid, so long as their own interests were not endangered. The representatives of these donor countries in the capital saw everything and knew everything, but did nothing that could be considered 'interference in the internal affairs of the Government.' Yet certain sections of the Western press would sometimes talk about the misuse of their taxpayers' money. More than once, Somalia was described in these circles as the graveyard of foreign aid.

Regarding the aid received by Somalia, there was an attitude of easy-come-easy-go. No one cared to invest such funds in production. Government just relaxed and consumed these funds. Anyone in a position to handle funds siphoned off as much as possible for himself, his relatives, his friends and acquaintances. National interests took a back seat.

After a relatively short period in the Government, a 31 year old politician of the time was said to have amassed 31 million Somali shillings, equivalent at the time to approximately $US 5 million. God knows if this was true, but it was the talk of the town and, at the very least it was a metaphor of how things were.

Certainly some people were provided a great deal of money in loans—loans that were never intended to be repayed.

In March 1967, the French Government organized a referendum to ascertain the wishes of the people of French Somaliland regarding self-determination. In spite of France's manipulation of the population, and exaggerating the statistics of minority ethnic sections, the people voted "No" to France. However that did not stop France from ignoring the result of the referendum—as Britain had done in an earlier instance—and subsequently changing the name of the territory from French Somaliland to the French Territory of the Afars and Issas.

The Issas were the predominant Somali clan population group in French Somaliland, whilst the Afars were non-Somali and a numerically smaller ethnic group until France engineered their migration into the territory from contiguous land in Ethiopia so as to rig the referendum. Then, having changed the referendum result, the French also changed the name of the territory so that all reference to 'Somali' was eliminated.

The Somali Government took the case, as it had done for Ogaden and the NFD, to every forum, but once again the response received was not sympathetic. At the Organization of African Unity for instance, there were those who supported the inherited colonial boundaries, who argued that if even one boundary issue in Africa was opened for debate, then the whole African continent would be plunged into conflict. Not one nation tried dispassionately to question the motives of the colonial powers in creating these borders, or to look at individual cases on merit. Even though the imperialists had left, we were stubbornly resisting the chance to undo their mischief and correct their mistakes.

Instead of showing any sign of improvement, the political integrity of the Somalis as a nation continued to deteriorate. Conflicts with our neighbours further deepened. We were at loggerheads with both Ethiopia and Kenya. Due to the machinations of the French Administration, Djibouti had been snatched away from Somalia. In our own naivete, we never laid claim to the island of Socotra. The dream of a Greater Somalia appeared to be receding. Nevertheless Somalia continued to advocate for the right to self-determination for Somali people under foreign rule.

Writing about the character of Mr. Egal, John Drysdale, a former advisor to the Somali Government said: 'Always keenly interested in the problem of "the Somali territories", he made up his mind while in opposition that only a fraternal approach to Somalia's neighbours could restore hope and bring about a solution. He saw that it was his role to make such an approach since his command of English and his Pan-Africanist outlook made it possible for him to communicate effectively with English-speaking Africa'.*

So Mohamed Ibrahim Egal flew to Kinshasa for the OAU Heads of State meeting, held there in September 1967. There he was the co-signatory, with Kenya, of a declaration which stated: 'Both Governments have expressed their desire to respect each other's sovereignty and territorial integrity in the spirit of Paragraph 3 of Article III of the OAU Charter.'**

In November 1967, he signed the famous *Arusha Memorandum of Agreement* with the Government of Kenya which appeared to many to be a sell-out of Somali territory and its people. The contents of the Memorandum were all weighted in favour of Kenya. Kenya wanted peace as much as we did, but they apparently succeeded in winning it without making any concessions. They had to spend millions, which their budget could ill afford, to maintain control of NFD territory. Since the area was inhabited by ethnic Somalis, the Kenyan Government had to establish garrisons and send soldiers and police personnel from Nairobi to govern and to keep the area secure and to combat the activities of the liberation fighters. The Arusha Agreement relieved them of that burden. Even had President Abdirashid and the Government of Mohamed Egal felt unable materially to continue supporting the struggle of the NFD Somalis, it was presumptuous of them to have signed such an agreement with Kenya. The people of the territory had not even delegated the

---

* *Case Studies in African Diplomacy,* Number II p.86, compiled by Dar-es-Salaam University

** IBID

power to the Government of Somalia to sign any agreement which effectively took away their right to self-determination.

It was possible to argue that what the Somali Government was doing on behalf of Somalis outside the Republic amounted to interference in the internal affairs of another country, but this was an argument for the other countries to emphasize, not one to which we could ever subscribe. From the very beginning, our neighbouring countries had known that our support to the Somalis under their control was for the freedom of those people and for their union with their motherland. This was the solemn pledge given by every Somali Government since Independence. Yet the Prime Minister had acted in a manner which was tantamount to renunciation of this fundamental Somali principle.

During the mid-1960s I was working in the newly created Somali National News Agency (SONNA). Initially, I was able to continue to use Italian as my working language, but not for long.

At the News Agency there was an Italian born Expert from the United Nations Educational, Scientific and Cultural Organization (UNESCO) whose job was to help set up the organizational structure, and train various levels of personnel to man the Agency. As an Adviser, he proposed that the official language of the Agency be changed from Italian to English. The Minister of Information, who was from former British Somaliland, agreed. This posed a serious challenge for me.

As I was very keen to continue working at the Agency, I had to do something about improving my English. It became a question of life and death for me. To continue at the Agency I would have to learn good English. Italian was being gradually replaced, not just here in the news agency. More and more, important documents of state were being drafted in English. I knew I would have to work very hard to survive in this English-speaking environment. It was out of necessity that I was eventually able to work in English and, at a later stage, I was appointed Acting Director of the Agency.

In SONNA, we selected, compiled and edited all the items of national and international news each day, for use in national radio news bulletins, and by the two daily newspapers *Il Corriere della Somalia* and *Sawt al Somal,* and the national English language weekly Somali News. It was very exciting work, and in the news agency we were just about the best informed people in the country on both local and international news events and political developments. Our news sources included international wire services like Reuters, ANSA, *Agence France Press* (AFP), and Tass; radio monitoring of a wide range of stations in Africa, the Middle East, BBC World Service, VOA, and Radio Moscow; daily news bulletins produced by the major diplomatic missions in Mogadishu, including *Hsinhua* from China, USIS, and *Novosti* (USSR); and for national news, we had a network of 'stringer' correspondents at all district headquarters, who sent telegrams via radio operators on items of local news from most parts of the country.

News agency work was high profile, highly political, and high risk. Once I described a transitional leader of one of the Somali territories under foreign rule as a "puppet." The item was broadcast over Radio Mogadishu in its afternoon bulletin. On listening to the broadcast, one of the Cabinet Ministers rushed to the news agency to enquire who had prepared the item. It was easy to verify this, since the practice was for the sub-editor's and typist's initials to be typed at the end of each item. I was not present, but a colleague told the Minister I would be back after dinner.

At about 9.00 p.m. while I was walking up the hill towards the Ministry of Information, where both the Agency and Radio Mogadishu were housed, I suddenly heard a vehicle screeching to a halt nearby. The man sitting in the car opened the door and asked me to enter. He was a Cabinet Minister. As soon as I entered the car, he asked me on what authority I had referred to the politician in the article as a puppet. I explained to him that the tone of the news item in question was in accord with Government policy, and that if there were any new developments affecting policy, this would be communicated by the Minister of Information and passed down the line to us. He drove on to the Agency.

I was disturbed by the interest the Minister evinced in this fairly routine news item; it did not feel quite right. As far as I knew, there had been no change in our policy towards the occupied territories and to local collaborators of the colonizing regimes. The Minister accompanied me inside. He removed a news handout from one of the out-trays which contained items intended for publication in the next day's morning papers. Before leaving, he had some warning words to say to me on politics and the responsibility of media persons. This was un-precedented. Even the Minister of Information did not intervene in our work in this way, but sent his directives down through his departmental directors.

As a postscript to this story, this same Cabinet Minister was shortly thereafter caught spying for a foreign country. He was charged and found guilty of treason, and sentenced to life imprisonment. He served more than a decade of the sentence before being released by the Revolutionary Government of Siad Barre. With him an official, a civil servant, was also found guilty of collaborating and was jailed on the same charges.

Besides being a member of the National News Agency, I was also 'moonlighting' as a stringer for an international news agency. The country's press was relatively free at this time, and many of us were doing extra pieces of journalism. Ninety-nine per cent of the time there was no conflict of interests, since we were sending out the same information that was being prepared for release through our own national media. But as with political leaders everywhere, our leaders were very sensitive to what the press said about them.

On one occasion, I sent a despatch to the international agency and the item went through the tele-printers all over the world, it was picked up and broadcast by a number of foreign radio stations. The item was a comment on a quarrel between the Prime Minister and his immediate predecessor. There was nothing in particular against the Prime Minister, but what he probably objected to was the corresponding publicity it achieved for his predecessor. Anyhow, the sender of the item was traced, and I was hauled over the coals for overstepping the bounds of a good civil servant I was told to either give up being a 'stringer' or resign from SONNA. I chose to stay with SONNA.

There was no good telephone link with the outside world in the sixties, and urgent messages were sent out of the country only via telegraph, not telephone. This radio telegraph system was the one we used for our news despatches. Copies of everything that was transmitted were kept by the Post Office's Radio Marina transmitting station which was situated at the top of Monopolio hill. Despatches of specific news items were therefore easily traceable. Additionally, journalists working for different

and competing news networks could check out the news copy
sent out by rival correspondents.

Relative press freedom we did have, but forces were at work to
try and control or muzzle free comment. Some of the foreign en-
voys bluntly told our leaders what they liked and what they did
not. Their countries were giving us aid, so maybe they presumed
it gave them the right to dictate what we should and should not
write. It often seemed that we were willing to accept their dic-
tates and advice without question, even when it was clearly to
our own detriment.

The story is told of how a country donated hundreds of tractors to improve the cultivation of maize. A second country told us
that if we began growing maize, it would cost us more than if we
bought maize from them with the assistance they were giving us.
The Minister in charge of agriculture agreed to the latter sugges-
tion and allowed the tractors to get rusty, boosting another
country's farming industry, instead of our own.

In these first few years we struggled not unsuccessfully with
a parliamentary democracy. We had changed our leadership
twice by the ballot and not by the bullet. Our parliament was full
of merchants and opportunists, but there were some others
among them more idealistic and committed to the big issues of
state. We had free speech and a lively press. It was the period of
large injections of foreign aid and the wooing of the New Africa
by both East and West. For the young Somalia there was hope,
and it looked as though our country was going to make it work.

But we were impatient to run before we could walk. And in
our hurry, some major dimensions of national life were being
neglected. Our educational system was elitist, and no vision was
being applied to the development of our agriculture, livestock
and fisheries as major planks of the economy; they continued in
the same way as when we inherited them from the colonialists. It
would take hard work to secure a firm base for these industries
and infrastructures, but we were too often distracted. We hoped
for quick fixes and easy options, like the discovery of oil or valuable minerals. While the dream of a Greater Somalia was and
would continue for another two decades to be a great unifying
force in our national consciousness, it undoubtedly also consumed much of our energy and resources. Chou En Lai had ob-

served in the mid-sixties that Africa was ripe for revolution, and indeed *coup d'états* were happening all around us, but so far Somalia had escaped.

CHAPTER VI

In London: My First Diplomatic Assignment

I was appointed Administrative and Press Attache at the Somali Embassy in London, and the Prime Minister's Secretariat directed the Ministry of Information to relieve me of my duties with immediate effect. My appointment was a surprise to many influential people and those who considered themselves the elite, not a few of whom had expected the appointment for themselves. The Somali Embassy in London then consisted of four members: an Ambassador, a Counsellor, a First Secretary and an Attache.

I was happy to be posted to our embassy in London as a diplomatic representative of my country. Of the four of us at the embassy, I alone was from former Italian Somaliland, the other three being from the former British Protectorate. I was to deal with administration, finance and press matters. I was already conversant with each aspect of the work from my earlier jobs at the General Post Office, the Parliament and the News Agency.

On 13 January 1968, the Ambassador, Ahmed Jama Abdille 'Jangali' and I arrived in London together. The Counsellor and the First Secretary had arrived earlier. They had arranged accommodation for us at a hotel called the Ambassador, near Euston tube station.

To begin with, I thought the 'ambassador' hotel was intended for embassies' people. The next morning when I went to the coffee-shop downstairs for breakfast the waiter asked me whether I wanted an English breakfast. I thought he could be assessing my attitude towards the UK, and that if I refused to order English Breakfast, I might offend the host country. Unfortunately, I had no idea what an English breakfast was. I answered in the affirmative.

When the waiter brought me eggs and bacon I was shocked

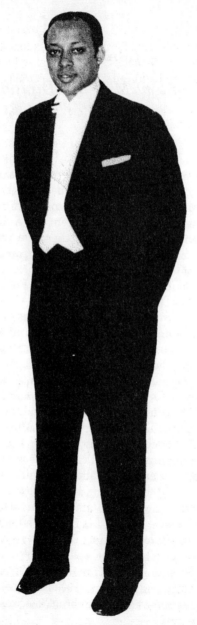

The Author as Diplomat in London.

and told him I did not eat pork. He replied that it was I who had ordered the English breakfast. He advised me to put the piece of bacon to the side of the plate. But as a Muslim I could not eat the eggs either, as they had been fried in the same pan and touched by the bacon. This the waiter could not understand at all. My dilemma was too difficult to explain, and I had to go without breakfast that first morning.

The Counsellor was an experienced person and knew London very well. For me, it was my first trip to London, although I had been to the United States of America and to several European countries while employed at the Press.

As our embassy had been closed down when Somalia broke off diplomatic relations with Britain in 1963, we had to look for new premises. Meanwhile, we used the office at the Italian Embassy which had looked after Somali interests during the period of the rupture. It was situated at Three Kings Yard, near Oxford Street. An Italian official was assigned to the office.

Italy was also taking care of Somali interests in other countries where Somalia did not have an established diplomatic mission. This practice was in accordance with an agreement concluded between the two countries on the day of our Independence.

Diplomatic relations with Britain had been restored at the end of 1967 after a lapse of four years, by the same person, Dr. Abdirashid Ali Shermarke, who had severed them, although he was now President of the Republic instead of Prime Minister. He had changed his policy, though the situation responsible for the rupture had not changed. In fact, there had been no indication of any change at all in Britain's attitude.

Prime Minister Mohamed Haji Ibrahim Egal was considered a pro-West leader. The Memorandum of Agreement he had signed in 1967 with Kenya was welcomed by the Western powers, especially Britain, while for Somali people on the whole, this Agreement was tantamount to renouncing our claim over the disputed territory and a betrayal of our national cause.

Although Abdirashid's regime concluded a Friendship Agreement which established a special relationship with the Soviet Union, our political system remained modeled on Western multi-party democracy. More than 80 political parties had participated in the preceding parliamentary elections, and the Western press viewed Somalia as one of the most democratic countries in Africa.

But Somalia was too democratic. The existence of so many parties was responsible for social tensions and conflict, a serious problem for a small country like ours. Everyone wanted to become a Member of Parliament. For political as well as financial reasons it was very important. The title of '*Onorevole*' or 'Honourable' was a potent symbol. Members of Parliament were treated very well by the Government, which met all their expenses including expenses incurred on 'political activities'.

People wanted to become members of parliament if only for the status and prestige. A well-known story of the time was of two persons—an MP and a rich merchant—who went to visit a Minister in his office. The peon on duty at the door of the Minister's office asked them their names. The MP said, "I'm Onorevole So-and-So." (Even if a person did not know Italian the title would always be uttered in that tongue—all the MPs would know how to say that word, even if they did not know how to write it.) The rich man, himself a well-known and established businessman of the city, gave his name as Haji So-and-So.

While the peon ushered the MP into the office of the Minister, he asked the other gentleman to sit in the waiting room. The honourable MP, who may very well have come to seek favours of the Minister, received VIP treatment, while the wealthy man, who may have come to discuss economic matters of potential significance to the country, had to wait in the Minister's ante room along with men of no account. To add insult to injury, a young boy with coffee and mineral water on a tray was seen passing through the waiting room to the Minister's office. It was clear that the Haji was going to have to wait for some time. The Ministerial habit of indulging in prolonged conversations with MPs over coffee was legendary; they did not care very much about the common people waiting outside.

Occasionally, laughter could be heard coming from the Minister's room. The rich man became increasingly angry. If he too had been an "Onorevole" he would not have been ignored for so long. What was more, he was wealthy enough to have 'bought' the constituencies of not just one but both of the men on the other side of the door.

The Haji resolved there and then to participate in the forthcoming parliamentary elections and ensure he did not suffer such indignities again. Sure enough, in the following elections the man did stand as a candidate, and got himself elected. It was rumoured that he paid each voter ten shillings to vote for him. The story may sound allegorical, but many Somalis are able to put a name to the main personage of the story. He was very well-known. When later he suceeding in being elected, he had no time to sit in the parliament. What he had wanted was to be called *onorevole* and promote his business interests, and he succeeded in his aims. Even within so-called democracies money can buy almost anything, including status.

The Government bore all the costs incurred by the ruling party candidates in their election campaigns. As in other underdeveloped countries where a large majority of the electorate are illiterate, the prospects for the ruling party in Somalia were always bright.

On one occasion which I remember, a minister invited some elders of Mogadishu to his residence, situated just behind the first line of villas on the *Via Lido*. He requested that they use their influence to persuade their people to vote for a particular candidate of the ruling SYL party. He told the elders that in return for extending support to the preferred candidate, the Government would allocate them a certain number of licenses for *taxi ape* the three-wheeled Vespa cab made in Italy, the most common and popular form of public transport in the city in the early independence years.

The elders who had been invited by the minister were not themselves going to ply those three-wheelers, but would pass the licenses on to members of their families, or sell them at a premium to others.

It was also common for the Government to offer import and export licenses to those who influenced public opinion, and these licenses too changed hands at a profit.

To return to my story, to be a diplomat was an excellent career. When I was told of my appointment I was thrilled. Many were jealous of me, particularly my young English-speaking compatriots who considered themselves more suitable or deserving of such a post than a person from the Italian side of the Republic. Though it was true I spoke Italian I also knew English, and Arabic, as well as Chinese and a little French. The job of a diplomat was, however, a new experience for me, and nobody thought we might require training before our postings abroad.

In London, it did not take us long to find suitable apartments. For the Ambassador, we found a good house in the Knightsbridge area. The First Secretary and I got an apartment at Gloucester Road, just above the tube station. The Counsellor took an apartment off Edgware Road, and for the Chancery we hired a large building at 60 Portland Place, near Regent's Park.

Soon after we settled down, I went to Foyles bookshop and bought the famous book on diplomacy by Satow, as well as a few other books on the same subject. The book by Sir Ernest Satow was *A Guide to Diplomatic Practice* and was to be studied by each of us to gain a grounding in the nature of the job that we had been assigned to perform.

The first paragraph of the book told us what we were supposed to do as diplomats. It said: 'Diplomacy is the application of intelligence and tact to the conduct of official relations between the governments of independent states, extending sometimes also to their relations with vassal states; or, more briefly still, the conduct of business between states by peaceful means'.

While books were useful guides to diplomatic functioning, most of our learning came through day-to-day experience. Every diplomat I met talked the same way, and asked more or less similar questions. They were interested in learning about the kind of commercial relations between the country one represents and the country in which one is currently posted.

There was a Diplomatic Association in London of which most diplomats were members. The Association organized a monthly lunch to which a VIP—such as a member of the Royal Family, or a high-ranking Government official, or a publisher from one of the newspapers—was invited as a special guest. Once, we had as guest of honour Lord Thomson of The Times of London, and I remember his remarks about people not being very interested in news about peace but much preferring to read about war, conflict, bloodshed and disasters, and how newspapers obliged by publishing what the readers wanted.

The Diplomatic Corps in London was extensive, and for us newcomers to the circle, exchange of views with such a range of diplomats from different countries was in itself a good training ground. Moreover, London was like a school for me; its daily newspapers, which carried articles on world politics and international conflicts, were as educative as contemporary text books on diplomacy.

In the sixties, there were a number of Somalis living in the U.K. These were concentrated in Cardiff, Birmingham, Liverpool and London. Those in London were concentrated in Aldgate East, a somewhat rundown working class area. Almost all of them were from former British Somaliland. A majority of those I saw in London's Aldgate East were seamen who had stayed on in London after retiring from their jobs with the merchant shipping fleets of Britain.

There was a Somali restaurant in the area where they would all gather. Sitting in the restaurant, they talked the whole day, sipping many cups of tea. The restaurant also cooked real Somali dishes, big pieces of boiled lamb's meat, and rice cooked with cinnamon and cardamom. With the exception of our Ambassador, we would all go there on Saturdays or Sundays to consume these home-style Somali dishes.

Although the Eastend Somalis had been there for twenty or thirty years, they behaved like people who had only just come from the homeland. They retained their national character and way of life, though mind you, many of them had travelled almost everywhere in the world.

These seamen told us tales of their experiences during sea voyages. They said they preferred the ships owned by the British and those of the Scandinavian companies, and complained about the Greek ships as being risky to travel in. They would regale us with stories of Somali seamen who were known to have been sailing on Greek ships but who had gone missing never to be seen again.

London was the home of many British officers and officials who had spent time in Somalia during the period of British Administration. There were others who had worked with the

Somali Government after independence. Together, they had formed an association known as the Anglo-Somali Society, some of whose members were considered authorities on Somali politics and society. A few of them had learned the Somali language while in Somalia, and spoke it fluently. Of these, the most renowned expert on the Somali language and culture was undoubtedly Dr B.W.'Goosh' Andrzejewski. He had devoted a great deal of his time and resources to collecting old and contemporary poetry and songs. He had personally translated many famous Somali poems and modern theatrical comedies. It was always a pleasure to visit his library at his home. J.Drysdale and I.M.Lewis are two more such well-known British experts on Somalia.

Some members of the society fondly reminisced about their life in the former Somaliland Protectorate, and spoke fondly of our people. But I often wondered about the depth of their concern, and whether this had been manifest while they were working in Somalia, or whether this retrospective affection was not nostalgia for a more glorious personal past. I believe some of them could have had considerable influence, but they had remained passive spectators to the injustices done against the Somalis.

The British Broadcasting Corporation's external services at Bush House also ran a Somali Service, a daily programme being beamed to Somali listeners all over the world. The news readers were Somalis. The programme coordinators and supervisors were British. As the Somali language had no script then, the news readers had to translate the news directly from the English text and, miraculously, they did this, without any written translation. At the actual time of the broadcast, they looked at the English text but announced it in Somali.

The Somali Service of the BBC gained a formidable reputation among Somalis, and it has retained this popularity and credibility with its audience to the present. Even in the nomadic areas of Somalia, people carried small transistor radios on their shoulders, while leading camels to and from the water wells. In the towns, people would gather around those teashops which had installed a loud speaker at their premises to relay the BBC programme. In their homes, people listened to it without fail. In short, the BBC's service was more popular than the national radio stations of Mogadishu and Hargeisa. Among the famous newsreaders were Osman Sugulle, Osman Hassan, Mustafa Haji Nur, Ahmed Ismail Samater, Hussein Mohamed Bullale, and Ismail Haji Abdi.

The Somalis' attachment to the BBC Somali Service is quite extraordinary. The Service since its inception in 1957 has served as Somalia's link with the world. Very few Somalis listened to Arabic or English language broadcasts, but everybody eagerly awaited 17:30 HRS and 21:00 HRS East African time, the two slots allocated for Somali transmissions. The signature tune for the Service is a piece of music from a well known patriotic song composed by Abdullahi Karshe:

Dadkaan dhawaaqaya,
Dhulkooda doonaya,
Haddey u dhiidhiyeen,
Allahayow u dhiib

These people who are raising their voice,
Who want their land;
As they struggle for it,
Oh Allah help them succeed.

Irrespective of the level of his education, a Somali will always be able to discuss knowledgeably on current political events in the world. Politics is a favourite national pastime. After listening to the BBC programme, people usually remain near the radio speakers to discuss and analyze what they have just heard.

When a Somali goes to buy a radio, he invariably asks the shopkeeper if the set can pick up the BBC. For most people, that is the criterion for buying a radio set. If visitors to the house of a friend see a radio on the table, they automatically ask if it 'catches the BBC', meaning the BBC Somali Service; meaning, is it a good quality short-wave set? Radio is a perfect communication medium for an oral society like ours.

To return once again to London, the building we rented for the embassy in Portland Place was a very peculiar house. One evening I read in a London evening newspaper that the Somali Embassy had rented a haunted house. The paper said that the Embassy of Cameroun had been there previously, but had moved out because it was believed there was a ghost in the building. I thought the article might be a practical joke or that it had something to do with Camerounian superstition and belief about voodoo. Sometimes, I too believe in such things. My office was at the end of the corridor on the ground floor. Above my office there was what I believed to be the office of the First Secretary. One night, while I was working late I suddenly heard footsteps of children and adults on the floor above my office. I stopped working and listened carefully. I definitely heard people moving back and forth above my head. Instantly, the article in the newspaper about the ghosts came to my mind and I said to myself, "It was true what the paper said…and why the Cameroun Embassy left the place." It was late, the First Secretary's office was already closed and I was alone in the embassy. I thought to myself, "If this is happening on the floor above it could also be happening in the basement."

For a moment I could not move. If the ghosts heard me make a noise, I thought, they might come down, and if they came down the stairs they would effectively block my way to the front door. Then I made a dash for it. I did not even cover the typewriter and calculator. I moved as quietly and quickly as possible and rushed out of the front door, took my little Fiat 850 car which was parked outside the embassy, and was off to Stanmore, Middlesex where I then lived, not stopping anywhere until I got home.

The next day, early in the morning, before anyone else arrived, I returned to the embassy to look the place over thoroughly. I first went round the outside of the building to where my office window faced on to the side street. Next to my window was a door with the number 60A Portland Place on it. Above the window of my office was a window which had curtains of a different colour from the ones in the embassy. There appeared to be an intervening floor between my window and the First Secretary's window at the top of the building. From inside the embassy this room was not visible, not accessible. It must be taking up space adjacent to our cypher room, but opening up to the the house at 60A. It was indeed occupied by someone else, but not a ghost. The newspaper had clearly not investigated the Camerounian claims before publishing what must be admitted was a good story.

CHAPTER VII

President Shermarke is Dead...

It was during my time in London when, on the evening of 15 October 1969, while I was watching the evening newscast on BBC Television at home, a shock headline appeared on the screen.

"President Shermarke is dead", the news reader announced. The TV showed a portrait of President Abdirashid Ali Shermarke, wearing his usual Brava-made hat. He had been the second President of the Somali Republic.

The report we received in London said that he had been shot dead by one of the guards responsible for his security. He had gone on a tour of the Northern Region of the Republic and at the time of his assassination had been in Las Anod District. The reason for the killing seemed to have been internal clan politics. The assassin was speedily dealt with—sentenced to death and executed by a firing squad in the same district where the killing had happened.

The Prime Minister, Mohamed Haji Ibrahim Egal was in the United States of America when news of the assassination broke. One of his wives, the younger one, was in London to buy dinner services and silverware for the Prime Minister's newly constructed villa—to be called Villa Egal and which was to have become their official residence. All the cutlery and crockery was to be embossed or engraved with the name of the villa.

Mr. Egal was 'resting' in the United States, having just completed an official visit there. He had to rush back to Mogadishu to attend the burial of the late President and prepare for the election of a new one.

Constitutionally, the President was to be elected by the National Assembly. The Somali Youth League as the ruling party had a comfortable majority in the Parliament. But there were many members who could not be relied upon to cast their vote along party lines unless they were properly persuaded. The person to be elected president would not only acquire prestige but would also reap financial returns for himself and for his own relatives and tribesmen. Personal interest took precedence over party and national interests. For the parliamentarians, their opportunity to make money and gain high office lay in how they would cast their vote.

Since Independence, nine years and three months had elapsed when Abdirashid was assassinated. During these nine years the SYL had ruled with an iron hand in a velvet glove. Although outsiders described the SYL government as democratic, it had always manipulated elections in its favour. The money the Party used for such purposes, to promote its own interests, was the same money which came to Somalia from foreign countries as aid for development. Unfortunately, such external assistance was largely being consumed by a small elite. Not surprising that our country had been dubbed the graveyard of foreign aid.

On the demise of Abdirashid too, the usual vested interests wanted to ensure that, after the funeral was over, the new President would be one who would continue the policies of his predecessor. The headquarters of the SYL was near the site called Dhagaxtuur, so named after the famous 1948 stone-throwing battle against the British during the Independence struggle. The place was now buzzing with all sorts of manoeuvering.

The Somali Youth League reached a consensus on their candidate for the next President. The consensus candidate had been arrived at after considerable canvassing and the inevitable horse-trading. One unconfirmed rumour said that every parliamentarian who agreed to vote for the designated candidate was to receive a sum of 100 thousand Somali shillings (equivalent to approximately $15000) apart from rewards consequent upon the successful election of the Party candidate. Parliament was scheduled to meet on the morning of 21 October 1969 to elect the next president.

At 3 o'clock in the morning of 21 October 1969 a group of Army Officers swooped down upon the residences of the Prime Minister and his cabinet colleagues, and removed them to unknown places. A former President, a former Prime Minister and certain other 'elder statesmen' were taken away by

Major General Mohamed Siad Barre:
after staging the coup in 1969.

First Charter of the Revolution.

21 OTTOBRE 1969

RIVOLUZIONE SENZA
SPARGIMENTO DI SANGUE

IN NOME DEL POPOLO SOMALO
IL CONSIGLIO RIVOLUZIONARIO SUPREMO

CONSAPEVOLE: DEL SACRO DIRITTO DEI POPOLI SOLENNEMENTE CONSACRATO NELLA CARTA DELLE NAZIONI UNITE E DELL'ORGANIZZAZIONE DELL'UNITA' AFRICANA;

DETERMINATO: A COLLABORARE CON TUTTI I POPOLI PER IL CONSOLIDAMENTO DELLA LIBERTA', DELLA GIUSTIZIA E DELLA PACE NEL MONDO, ED IN PARTICOLARE CON I POPOLI AMANTI DELLA PACE E DELLA GIUSTIZIA SOCIALE;

FERMAMENTE: DECISO A CONSOLIDARE E TUTELARE L'INDIPENDENZA DELLA NAZIONE SOMALA E PER CREARE UNA SOCIETA' FONDATA SULLA SOVRANITA' POPOLARE E SULL'UGUAGLIANZA DEI DIRITTI E DEI DOVERI DI TUTTI I CITTADINI SENZA DISTINZIONE DI SESSO E DI CONDIZIONE SOCIALE.

DICHIARA

A: POLITICA INTERNA

1. — Costituire una società basata sul lavoro e sul principio della giustizia sociale, considerando le particolarità dell'ambiente e delle condizioni del popolo;

2. — Preparare e orientare lo sviluppo economico, sociale e culturale per raggiungere un rapido progresso del Paese;

3. — Liquidare l'analfabetismo e sviluppare il patrimonio culturale del popolo somalo;

4. — Costituire, con priorità, le condizioni di base per la scrittura della lingua somala;

5. — Liquidare la corruzione, l'anarchia, il tribalismo ed ogni altro fenomeno di malcostume sociale nell'attività statale;

6. — Abolire i partiti politici;

7. — Indire, nel momento opportuno, un'elezione popolare con assoluta imparzialità.

B: POLITICA ESTERA

1. — Appoggiare la solidarietà internazionale ed i movimenti di liberazione nazionale;

2. — Lottare contro ogni forma di colonialismo e neocolonialismo;

3. — Lottare per l'unità della Nazione Somala;

4. — Riconoscere pienamente il principio della coesistenza pacifica tra tutti i popoli;

5. — Proseguire la via della politica della neutralità positiva;

6. — Rispettare e riconoscere tutti gli impegni internazionali precedentemente conclusi dalla Repubblica Somala.

the Army. The Government of Prime Minister Egal had been overthrown inwhat was described by its perpetrators as "A Bloodless Revolution." Reports reaching us in London told of how the people had welcomed the 'Revolution' and had poured onto the streets of Mogadishu to support it.

Since Independence, the growing corruption, nepotism and total disregard for the common man had driven the people to a point where they would have welcomed any change. They believed anything would be better than the situation prevailing in the country. The new Revolutionary Council's declaration, therefore, to restore justice and equality before the law, to uphold the right to work, the people's right to run their own affairs, fair distribution of the nation's income, eradication of hunger, disease and ignorance, and to eliminate the insidious but prevalent system of tribalism was very welcome.

On the morning of 21 October 1969, the Parliament's doors were locked and the Supreme Revolutionary Council took over the governance of the country at gun-point. The Revolution's symbol was a gun and a hand, and in the background the Koran. This symbol appeared on the First Charter of the Revolution, with a headline in bold capital letters which read: "21st October 1969, Bloodless Revolution."

A year later, when the Supreme Revolutionary Council issued the Second Charter, the Koran and other symbols were gone, and the declaration was: 'as from October 21, 1970, the Somali Democratic Republic will adopt Scientific Socialism'. The Supreme Revolutionary Council which had taken over power was composed of 23 members, headed by Major General Mohamed Siad Barre as President.

In June 1971, I was transferred to Beijing, capital of the People's Republic of China. After three and a half years in London, where the pace of life was extremely fast, I arrived in Beijing to find that time had almost stopped. Everything seemed to be happening in slow motion. In a letter to a friend in London, I wrote of my first impressions of China, especially Beijing, remarking that it was very difficult not to get bored during off duty hours. Everything was very different to what I had experienced in London. As I had arrived in China just after the Cultural Revolution, I observed significant differences in the people's behaviour from when I had been there as a student in the early sixties. For a start they were more disciplined than I remembered. During the sixties, the Chinese government invited many people from African, Asian and Latin American countries to visit their country, through links with political parties, Youth, and Friendship organizations. The People's Republic of China then was not a member of the United Nations, its seat occupied by Taiwan. The people of Africa, Asia and Latin America were, by and large, sympathetic to the aspirations of the people of China. But, in view of the American opposition, their sympathies were of no avail as far as China's admission to the UN was concerned. Since its independence in 1948, the People's Republic of China had been trying to establish friendly links with almost all countries, including countries which consistently voted against UN resolutions seeking China's admission to the world body.

I found it difficult to understand the attitude of the countries objecting to China's admission to the United Nations. How could these countries support Taiwan with a population of 15 million Chinese against the People's Republic, a country of more than 800 million? It was beyond my comprehension. In politics, it seemed, emotions and brute power had more place than justice and humanitarianism.

Nothing stays the same forever, and this was true for China. Eventually, the world recognized China as a country. The day US President, Richard Nixon came to China in the early seventies, I watched the fleet of limousines carrying the President and retinue of a country once dubbed by China and until recently called 'a paper tiger'. I listened on my little transistor radio to the Voice of America commentary on Nixon's visit. The Americans had deployed two earth satellites, one over Beijing and the other over Shanghai, to facilitate direct transmission of Nixon's visit.

The visit marked the end of isolation for the country of Mao Tse Tung and Chou En Lai. The Chinese believed that they had won the game as the American leaders had first come to visit their country, and not the other way round. It appeared as if the Americans were very eager to open a relationship with the People's Republic, while they pretended to minimize its importance.

Second Charter of the Revolution.

REPUBBLICA DEMOCRATICA SOMALA

PRESIDENZA DEL CONSIGLIO RIVOLUZIONARIO SUPREMO

SECONDA CARTA DELLA RIVOLUZIONE

————oOo————

IL PRESIDENTE

del CONSIGLIO RIVOLUZIONARIO SUPREMO

VISTO la Prima Carta della Rivoluzione del 21 Ottobre 1969 che stabilisce la politica interna ed estera della Repubblica Democratica Somala;

CONSIDERATO la necessità di chiarire ulteriormente gli obiettivi dello Stato;

PRESO NOTA dell'approvazione del Consiglio Rivoluzionario Supremo;

DICHIARA

che,

poichè la Prima Carta della Rivoluzione stabilisce che lo scopo basilare dello Stato è quello di creare una società basata sul Lavoro e sui principii della giustizia sociale;

e che,

considerato che il Socialismo è l'unico sistema filosofico che aiuterà a formare detta società;

la REPUBBLICA DEMOCRATICA SOMALA ha, con effetto dal 21 Ottobre 1970, adottato il SOCIALISMO SCIENTIFICO come suo ambito traguardo;

e adotterà qualsiasi passo necessario per la sua piena attuazione per il progresso e la prosperità del Popolo Somalo.

Mogadiscio, Gennaio 1971

IL PRESIDENTE
del CONSIGLIO RIVOLUZIONARIO SUPREMO
Gen. di Div. Mohamed Siad Barre

The Supreme Revolutionary Council Members and Civilian Members of the Government, during the early period.

Soon after President Nixon's visit, diplomats in Beijing noted an extreme shortage of the popular Chinese liqueur, Mou Tai. It was even missing from the usual round of cocktail parties given by the diplomatic missions. The story was that Nixon and his delegation had acquired the taste for Mou Tai and had bought up virtually all available stocks and left the country dry.

Although the Chinese needed Western technology, they never allowed the Western countries to dominate them. As far as possible they tried to maintain their national dignity. One could not but admire the way the Chinese were dealing with a difficult situation. They were candid about the conditions which prevailed in China and often told us that they were a poor and under-developed country. For me, China has been a great country, successfully managing to provide food and other basic necessities to its hundreds of millions of people. Their success was a miracle.

The people we saw in the streets and in the supermarkets were always full of cheer. They were healthy and physically strong. Their physical fitness was in part due to their habit of doing regular exercise. Every morning at 10 o'clock most Chinese would exercise to the music of Radio Beijing. At the familiar signal, all activity would come to a standstill. Officials and students and workers on their way to work would alight from their bicycles. Work in hospitals and government offices virtually came to a stop. For the ten minutes during which the special tune for physical exercises was played, people everywhere performed their daily fitness routine. Physical training constituted an important aspect of the teachings of Chairman Mao Tse Tung, one of whose sayings was: *Duanlian shenti baawey zuguo:* A healthy body protects the country.

I happened to see Chairman Mao only once from a distance, standing on the balcony at Tian An Men Square, above the gate to the Forbidden City—known in Chinese as "Tien An Men Chen Low." I did, however, have the opportunity to meet Chou En Lai on several occasions. He attended the various National Day functions at the different embassies.

Somalia's relations with China were classed as very cordial, in spite of the close ties existing between Somalia and the Soviet Union, and Chou En Lai evinced a special interest in and

warmth towards our people. It was during his official visit to
Somalia in 1964 that Chou made his famous remarks about
Africa being ready for revolution. Everywhere in Mogadishu, the
masses had been out to greet him. A song, 'Long live the friendship
between the peoples of China and Somalia' and 'Long live Chou
en Lai, down with his enemies,' were composed and played constantly on national radio in honour of his visit.

During my posting in China the President of the Somali
Democratic Republic was invited to visit China. Our Ambassador called on Premier Chou En Lai to discuss the visit, and I
accompanied him to that meeting. When we had finished discussing the proposed programme for the visit, Premier Chou Lai
and the Ambassador began talking about more general subjects.

Chou said to the Ambassador, "Why don't you stop your
friends from stealing your marine resources?" He did not specify
who was meant by 'your friends', but it was very clear to us that
he was referring to the Russians with whom, it was true, we had
good relations. Somalia at the time was one of a number of
African countries in the Soviet camp. Some quarters even commented that, Somalia was the bridge for communist penetration
into Africa. The Soviets were indeed lifting huge amount of fish
from our waters as if they owned them. We smiled and told the
Chinese Premier that we did not think we were in a position to
stop them.

Chou En Lai, small in stature, was in his way a giant. He followed everything that was happening in the world and was
reputed to spend long hours a day working tirelessly for his
country. Once, a journalist who was interviewing him late at
night, asked him: "Mr. Prime Minister, when do you sleep?"

The answer came, "While the interpreter is translating what
I have said in Chinese, I close my eyes and sleep."

He also spoke many foreign languages and did not really need
an interpreter, though he always preferred to use one.

We agreed with Chou En Lai that the news of the visit of the
Somali President would be announced simultaneously from
Beijing and Mogadishu. Until then, it was to be kept confiden-
tial. But a short while later, a person from a country that should
have been the last to know of the visit, commented to me at a
cocktail party, "So your President is coming to China".

This was a shock to me. I knew the Chinese would not have given this information to anyone. I myself had not spoken to anyone on the subject either. My Ambassador was present at the function, and was standing at the other end of the Hall. I went to him and asked him if he had spoken about the President's visit to anyone. He too said he had not. I wondered who else could have leaked the information. The embassy sent a coded message to our Foreign Ministry asking if they had made the announcement. No reply. That was also unusual. The 'mole' must have been there at home.

The President made his official visit to China in 1972. He had talks with Premier Chou En Lai and other officials, but the scheduled meeting with Chairman Mao Tse Tung could not take place. We waited up the whole night, until the early morning hours. The Chairman was not feeling well. It was clear to us that the Chinese were really trying to arrange the meeting but were ultimately unable. We thought he must be very sick, otherwise they would have organized a hand-shaking meeting at least for the photographers. This was also important for our prestige as it was a very essential part of the protocol for a visiting Head of State.

After his visit to China, the President went on to the Democratic People's Republic of Korea. At the airport in Pyongyang, the Somali delegation, of which I was also a member, was received by the DPRK's 'Great Leader' Kim Il Sung, and other important North Korean personages. In addition, hundreds of people had lined the streets, right from the airport to the Palace, to welcome the Somali President.

The DPRK was even more isolated than China. Their contacts with the outside world were very limited. There were barely half a dozen foreign embassies in Pyongyang. Their communications with the world passed through the Soviet Union and the People's Republic of China only. In Pyongyang, the stamp of Kim II Sung was discernible on everything. In a word, Kim Il Sung was the DPRK, and vice versa. All statements began with praise to the 'Great Leader of the 40 million Korean people', i.e. the population of both the Koreas, North and South.

The programme of the Somali President's visit included a tour of the Museum of Kim Il Sung which contained wall to wall photographs of Kim in every one of over fifty rooms, and the members of our delegation had to look at them all. The Korean protocol officers who accompanied us were clearly nervous, fearing possibly that the Somalis would not wish to go round the whole museum; how would they explain that to their bosses? For us it was very difficult to maintain an interest in everything they wished us to see. For them, it was a fundamental duty to show and explain all the 'great achievements of the Korean people under Kim Il Sung'. Everywhere Kim Il Sung had put his feet had been transformed into national monuments, and visitors were obliged to see them all.

The Korean protocol arrangements were somewhat strange. For instance, the Korean Leader was to host a dinner in honour of our visiting delegation at 20:00 hours one evening. No sooner had we returned to the guest house at 17:00 hours from a tour of various economic projects than a protocol officer informed me that the Somali President should be ready at 18:00 hours. "For what?" I asked. In reply, he just repeated what he had said earlier.

As far as we knew there was no other engagement until the dinner, but it appeared they were asking us to be there two hours early, and we complied. The thought crossed our minds that perhaps Kim Il Sung wanted to hold further talks with the President before dinner. At 6 o'clock sharp, our President and his entourage arrived at the designated place for the dinner. We were seated in a hall and requested to wait. A huge colour portrait of The Great Leader in the center of the Hall was the only visible decoration in the room. I noticed three or four foreigners sitting in another part of the Hall. I was curious to know who they were, so I went over and spoke to one of them. He was a diplomat from a Middle Eastern country. He told me that he and the others were invited guests at the dinner arranged in our honour. They had also been asked to come at the revised time of 6 o'clock. We never found out why our arrival for dinner had been advanced, for we were kept waiting for the next two hours before the dinner commenced.

The Koreans were so confident of their security and safety arrangements for VIP guests that the doors at the guest house had no locks! The only problem was that you could not yourself feel at ease in your room. To keep it closed at night, some of us placed a chair or writing table behind the door.

Once, when the President was free, he wanted some exercise. He was well known for his love of table-tennis, and there was a table in one of the halls at the guest house. He asked me to play with him, assuming that as I was posted in China I should be able to play good ping pong—which was not the case. At one point, I do not remember in what connection, I addressed him as usual as Excellency, Mr. President. He looked at me and said, "You're not yet a revolutionary. Call me Jaalle."

The word *jaalle* was new to me, because when it was adopted I had been out of the country. The word, an old Somali word, had been re-activated by the Revolutionary Government and, over the years, it became so inextricably linked with that period of our history that it is no longer a comfortable word to use. It has been banished.

The protocol department in the Ministry of Foreign Affairs in Mogadishu had prepared gifts to be presented by the visiting President to the leaders of Korea, decorative items made of ivory. On one of these gifts, our protocol department had put the name of Kim Il Sung. It was a little smaller than another, meant for the President of Korea who, although unknown to the world, was the higher in rank. Before their presentation I wanted to show them to the Korean Protocol Officer in charge of our programme. When he saw that the Kim Il Sung piece was smaller than the other he was most alarmed.

"No, No, No," he said, "Comrade Kim must be given the bigger one."

Protocol-wise we were correct, but in Pyongyang protocol was proper only when Comrade Kim was happy. I asked him to bring me a knife and some glue, and I interchanged the name plates on the gifts. The protocol officer was overwhelmingly grateful at being rescued from a crisis of terrible proportions. I was almost moved to shout "Long live Kim Il Sung!"

Our visit concluded on a successful note. The Somalis were highly impressed by the agricultural development and the artificial lakes of North Korea. In the field of technology, the Koreans had done well, and they were keen to share their expertise with other developing countries, to win friends and influence people.

The application of Kim Il Sung's ideas was called the Juche Idea, and the North Koreans were keen to export their approach to social mobilization, but they lacked the resources to influence through aid. They could, however, supply some materials and technical personnel, with the recipient country providing the money to pay the workers and providing the hard currency if other materials were needed from a third country.

The Presidential delegation left for home and I returned to my post in China.

The Juche Idea, the DPRK's version of socialist self-reliance, made a brief appearance in Somalia following this visit. Its trappings included the appearance of larger-than-life size full-length paintings of the Somali President looking for all the world like Kim Il Sung, except for the face.

A few months later I was called back home to undergo a three-month training course in a military camp, as every civil servant was obliged to do under the new edicts. The Camp was intended by the Revolutionary Government to re-educate or brain-wash civil servants, specially those who had been trained in non-socialist countries. The purpose of the camp, according to the Government, was to eliminate the different foreign cultural influences and to assert the Somali culture. Those civil servants who had received their education in Western Europe were considered particularly harmful to the socialist ideology that the Revolution was trying to promote. The camp was also to train everyone in government service to handle a rifle, in other words to indirectly introduce a national service programme.

Ambassadors and high-ranking officials in the Government had already done the course. In my intake group were First Secretaries from various Somali Embassies abroad, school directors and teachers.

When I arrived in Mogadishu, the three month programme had already begun. It was like going to boarding school. I took with me a small bag containing a few items of clothing and toiletries. Upon arrival at the camp office I was told to go to barrack room no. 4. As I reached the door of the barracks I recognized some friends and familiar faces. They were all wearing boots and khaki uniforms like soldiers. An Inspector accompanied them. I had been forewarned by those who had already completed the course, that discipline was strict and that I must appear serious, especially when the camp staff were nearby.

"Put your bag down," said the Inspector. I put my bag down.

"Collect the cigarette butts and used matchsticks from outside the door," he ordered me.

I got down on my knees on the sandy ground he had indicated and began collecting the butts and half burnt pieces of wood with my right hand and placed them in my left hand. I looked up at my colleagues who were standing there with the Inspector, and could read from their faces that they were enjoying every minute of this. Eventually the Inspector appeared satisfied that I was prepared to obey orders, and told me I could stop. He showed me my bed, which was an upper bunk. Next I was taken to a store room where thousands of old khaki uniforms and boots of all sizes were stored. I selected items to fit me, and the storekeeper gave me a set of brass buttons for the shirts.

The camp was on the outskirts of the capital, beyond the airport. It was originally called *Campo Bottego,* and had been an Italian military camp. After the Revolution, its name was changed to Halane, after a young Somali soldier who had died for the country during the war against Ethiopia in 1964.

Every morning at 04:30, we had to be up and ready for running and other physical exercises which were the routine until 06:00. At 06:30 we had breakfast, at 07:00, dressed in army gear, all of us stood in line while a corporal checked the cleanliness of our uniforms, neatness, correctness and shininess of our boots and buttons. We were required to go to classes next. The teaching content was socialist ideology and military related matters. From time to time trainees would deliver lectures on subjects of their choice or specialization, so long as they avoided saying anything against socialism. In the afternoons we sat outside the barrack and polished boots and brasses.

As a result of morning exercise, many previously over-weight civil servants became more physically fit and active than they had been for years. There was good camaraderie among the camp inmates, and a chance to make new friends and meet old colleagues whom one had not seen for a very long time. Yet it is hard to identify any positive benefits of the experiment beyond this.

One morning, while walking by the office building of the

camp, I saw one of the clerks holding a copy of the English-language daily newspaper *The October Star.* A bold headline on the front page said "Ours is Marxism-Leninism." The Revolution was only three years old then. How fast our rulers were learning the history of socialism! Only two years earlier, the Supreme Revolutionary Council, the country's highest body, had issued the Second Charter of the Revolution declaring that the country's system would be based on Scientific Socialism.

Those who were lecturing us on socialism and communism were now telling us that socialism was a transitional phase on the path towards communism, the attainment of which would take a long time. Even the Russians had not yet realized that utopia.

When the Second Charter was issued, the President of the Supreme Revolutionary Council declared that we had chosen the path of scientific socialism because it was the only route to rapid transformation of the country into a developed and economically advanced nation.

Socialism was not a bad idea. It was a means to social and economic progress. It encouraged people to participate and made them feel that they would share both the burdens and the benefits. But what of the next step, communism. Could a Somali be a Communist? Communism was an ideology that affected religious belief. All our people were Muslims, and the communist ideology preaches atheism.

The President of the Supreme Revolutionary Council, Mohamed Siad Barre, who ceaselessly spoke on socialism and communism may never even have read a book on these subjects. He certainly had not been to a school where it was taught. But he wanted to teach it to the people of Somalia. That was true of other members of the SRC, most of whom had no idea what they were trying to introduce in the country. The Supreme Revolutionary Council nevertheless resolved that all the people must be re-educated. A political office was created—*Xafiiska Xirirka Dadweynahe,* Public Relations Office, which later became the *Xafiiska Siyaasadda* or Political Office. This office was entrusted with the task of promoting the policy of the revolutionary government. To do this, it established centres for so-called orientation throughout the country and deputed a representative to each Orientation Centre once a week, to address the people gathered there. These representatives spoke on such topics as the corruption that had prevailed before the Revolution, the aims of the Revolution, and the advantages of the Socialist system introduced by the Revolutionary regime. At these weekly Centre meetings, in presence of the representatives of the Political Office, the people listened very attentively to what the speakers said.

By and large, what they had to say about previous governments was true. Undoubtedly, corruption, malpractice, misuse of state property, tribalism and nepotism were all common during the nine years that preceded the Revolution. All this was known to the people, only in the past they had felt helpless. Now, the representatives of the revolutionary regime were saying that in future Somali society would never suffer from such evils.

The Political Office was also responsible for the display of posters on big billboards along the main streets, and for the big portraits of the President which were put up in front of all government buildings. The style of this art, I think, is called neo-realism, and was the fashion in all the socialist Eastern Bloc countries during the period, and in those countries of Africa, Asia and Latin America which were under the patronage of the Soviet Union, as distinct from those influenced by the United States of America. Slogans in praise of our brand of socialism were writ large on the walls of buildings, both public and private, along with anti-imperialist slogans. I recall a poster which showed a person with grotesque features extracting blood with a syringe from a rather normal person. Another depicted a snake sucking the blood of a man. One was left in no doubt which figures represented the imperialists, or the deposed government, in these works.

The new Government also created an organization called the National Security Service (NSS) or *Nabad Suggidda Somaliyeed,* which was entrusted with the task of suppressing ant-revolutionary activities.

In the past the people had been able to speak with complete freedom. In the revolutionary era, the people could neither speak nor do, anything but what was taught and permitted by the Revolution.

The Revolution promised to restore the dignity of the nation and the country. To demonstrate his independent attitude, the President rejected a request from an important quarter to stop ships which flew the Somali flag as a flag of convenience, from visiting the ports of Havana and Hanoi. In retaliation, financial assistance to Somalia was stopped. The President also decided to accord recognition to the German Democratic Republic. Contrary to what the Federal Republic did with some other countries that had recognized East Germany, it did not break off diplomatic relations with Somalia. It did, however, stop certain economic assistance it had been giving Somalia, though assistance to the police force continued as usual. The Ambassadors from both Germanies were present in Mogadishu at the same time.

In due course of time, the Political Office began functioning like a political party, directing all its branches to organize weekly meetings of civil servants and of the ordinary people. Anyone who did not participate in these meetings was considered antrevolutionary. Everybody was obliged to go to the Orientation Centres. At the end of each meeting, participants stood up and sang a revolutionary song dedicated to the President of the Supreme Revolutionary Council, Major General Mohamed Siad Barre. This one is the most famous of all the songs composed for the glorification of Siad:

Guul wade Siad	The Victorious Siad
Abahii Garashada	The Father of Knowledge
Gaygayagow	Of our Lands
Hantiwadaagga waa	Socialism is the system
Habkaa	That leads us to
Barwaaqo noo	prosperity
horseedayee	This tumult
Bullaankan baxaaya	This light which is
Nuurkaan bidhaamaya	illuminating
Dhawaaqa oo isu baqaya	This unified call
Waa Barbaarta iyo	Are the Youth and
shaqaalaha	Workers
Oo is biirsaday	That are united
Bar-bar taagan	Who support
Towraddooda	Their Revolution's
Ra'yigii ka soo baxa	Directives
Oo ballan qaaday	That promise
Ha..Ha	Ha..Ha
Hantiwadaag inay	To defend Socialism.
badbaadiyaan	

The speeches delivered at the weekly meetings usually included praise of the President, who was most usually referred to as The Father of the Nation, but also as the Leader, the Untiring, the Light of Africa and other such glowing epithets. Whenever his name was mentioned, everyone applauded, and there were groups of women who would beat drums and ululate (which is to make a high-pitched acclamatory sound by rapidly vibrating the tongue against the lips while expelling air through the mouth). There were special groups of people at each Centre who were trained to interrupt the speeches with songs dedicated to the President, and phrases such as 'long live Siad', the speakers waiting until the interruption was over before continuing. The President's portrait and quotations from his speeches decorated the walls of all the neighbourhood Centres, as well as meeting rooms at the ministries, which were used for orientation purposes.

Shopkeepers were fined if they did not have the official portrait of the President on the walls of their shops. Such omissions were considered as ant-revolutionary gestures. Plain clothes security officers, victory pioneers called *guulwadeyaal,* and municipality guards were all in a position to threaten a shopkeeper whose Presidential portrait was 'not in conformity with the President's dignity', which often meant there was a spot or a mark on the glass or the frame.

CHAPTER VIII

At the Protocol Department

After my training in Halane Camp, I was initially among those who were told to return to their respective places of work, my last posting being Beijing. But then, someone decided otherwise, and I was told to report at the Ministry of Foreign Affairs, Department of Protocol.

The whole Ministry was housed in a very small building. At the Department of Protocol there were three officials of civil service grade A, myself grade B, and a lady who was grade C. The female colleague had more experience than all of us in dealing with diplomats. She knew all there was to know in the Department. She was quiet and hardworking.

I had once been grade A-6 in the establishment of the government of Abdirizak Haji Hussein in 1965, when I was acting-head of the Somali National News Agency (SONNA) in the Ministry of Information. Prime Minister Abdirizak Haji Hussein used to give annual merit awards to civil servants for hard work. The recipient of the award was named 'man of the year'. In 1965 one person was chosen from the Ministry of Finance and presented with So. Shs. 10.000, and in the Ministry of Information the same title was conferred on me, and I was given a trip abroad, accompanying the Minister of Information to the United States on an official visit. When I returned from the trip, I was told that my grade had been lowered to grade B-7. I protested to the Minister but nothing came out of it. Seven years later I was still grade B-7, working as Chief of Protocol, an important post anywhere in the world. My three A-6 colleagues were more entitled to the post than I, and I was willing for them to claim it. However, none of them showed any sign of wanting the responsibility. All three had been to the Soviet Union for education, two of them could barely read or write a document in English or Italian—the two languages most commonly used for government business—and so, I suppose, were reluctant to expose their inadequacies.

When I thought it was appropriate for me to fight for my right, which I had lost in 1965, I went to the Minister of Foreign Affairs who was already aware of my competence. He also knew the others in my Department. The Minister had known me since the days when I was working in the Ministry of Information. In those days he had been a diplomat, and whenever he came to Mogadishu for consultations he would visit the Ministry of Information to collect news of international events. The conversation between us went something like this:

Minister: Yes, Jaalle.

Me: *Maalin wanaagsan, Jaalle Wasiir.* (Good day Comrade Minister.)

Minister: Sit down. (pause) Yes, what is it?

He was from former British Somaliland, and liked speaking in English. Although he did not know Italian, his Arabic also was perfect. I started by expressing my appreciation at being appointed Chief of Protocol, and assured him that I would discharge my work without reservation.

After the preliminaries were over, I said to him, "Comrade Minister, I am Chief of Protocol, I am grade B-7, and yet my subordinates are all three of them grade A, and graduates in international law from the Soviet Union. If the people I am supposed to order are senior to me in grade, how can I demand work of them. I am ready to work under any one of them, or otherwise, if I'm to remain in post I should be given the grade which the post carries."

He knew as well as I that no matter what their degrees, the men in question could not do my job. His answer came. "You have been appointed by the President of the Supreme Revolutionary Council. This is the Revolutionary Era, and if you are seen fit to be appointed to a post, it doesn't matter what your grade is."

So, I did not get my 'promotion' and, by invoking the Revolution, the Minister was off the hook. I could not challenge it.

Anyhow, I continued doing my job with some pleasure and satisfaction. The Department was a very busy one. It had constant dealings with members of the diplomatic corps, looking after their privileges and immunities, such things as the importation of duty-free goods and diplomats' movements within the country. Diplomats were not allowed to go beyond 30 km. from the capital. Those who wished to had to come to us. We were 'the front office' for receiving and granting requests, though their requests were actually processed and cleared by the Ministry of the Interior and the National Security Service. Some Diplomats protested that this restriction on their movements violated the Vienna Convention.

The Revolutionary regime was very sensitive about the movements of foreigners, particularly Westerners. Whenever the latter tried to be difficult, we had to deal with them. We told them that we had the highest regard for their own safety and that our procedures were meant to ensure that. We told them that the restrictions were necessary for reasons of state security. Interestingly, both sides—the Ministry and the Diplomatic Missions—would refer to Article 26 of the Vienna Convention at times of dispute, and both sides used it to support their case. The Diplomats quoted the second part of the sentence which said, '…the receiving State shall ensure to all members of the mission, freedom of movement and travel in its territory'. The Ministry quoted the first sentence of the same article which said, 'Subject to its laws and regulations concerning zones entry into which is prohibited or regulated for reasons of national security…'.

The complete Article reads as follows:

> Article 26. Subject to its laws and regulations concerning zones entry into which is prohibited or regulated for reasons of national security, the receiving State shall ensure to all members of the mission freedom of movement and travel in its territory.

The government adopted strong measures against those who attempted to undermine its policy, and the people were really afraid even to talk to each other. Anyone who was found talking to a foreigner was subject to stringent punishment. I had been outside the country for the first two years of the Revolutionary era, and I did not realize the extent of fear the people felt until one day, when I happened to go to the coffee shop of the Croce del Sud Hotel which, as usual, was packed at mid-morning with customers. I happened to be with a foreigner who was an old acquaintance of mine, and whom I had bumped into and invited to have coffee with me. The bar was run Italian-style. So, conversing together we first approached the cashier. Having paid for our coffee, we turned to the counter behind us to collect our drinks only to find that there was nobody in the shop. Literally everybody had left the place and I found myself alone with the foreigner. Only the cashier and the two bar attendants had not forsaken the place.

At that moment, I realized the risk I was taking and the potential gravity of the situation. Unlikely as it was that the people present in the coffee-shop would have been arrested, they were afraid even to be called as witnesses in case I was arrested. The irony was that not only had it been quite normal for me to talk with anyone at all while I was abroad, it had constituted part of my duty as a diplomat to converse with foreigners.

When my companion looked around, he too was surprised. In the space of a minute the coffee house had been abandoned, half empty cups of coffee and tea left standing on the tables. God only knows what he thought; he probably expected some major trouble impending for me.

When he left after finishing his coffee, people began returning to the bar. However, I knew for the first time something that I would become very familiar with—the feeling of apprehension when in public places, that security persons, reputed to be present everywhere, might be watching and reporting on you. Though nothing actually happened this time, acquaintances advised me to be careful about meeting with foreigners if I wanted to stay in circulation.

Suspicion was rampant throughout the system. The NSS mentality was that foreigners were in the country to get news from and adversely influence the Somalis. It never occurred to them that the Somalis could also gain useful information from the foreigners. The government did not trust its own people, and the government was all-powerful. This was the recipe for our brand of social development.

My experience of totalitarian countries has been that people will compensate for the suffocation and monotony imposed by the system by satirizing the regime and making jokes about it. Somalis were no exception. I cite only one of the many telling jokes which were floating about Mogadishu at the time.

A *Reer Hamar,* a native of Mogadishu, dreamt that the Revolution had collapsed, and in the morning he told the story to someone. Within hours he was arrested by the NSS and taken to the torture chamber. After a few days he was released. Some short time later, while returning home from the mosque after offering his evening prayers, he met the same security man who had beaten him up while in custody.

Security Man: "Hey, Muridi, come here. Have you been having any more dreams?"

Muridi: "Don't I first need to sleep?"

The Revolutionary regime believed that by adopting strong arm tactics the people would become disciplined and made to work. To this end, there was forced mobilization of everybody. Even the children were not spared. Street children and youths were collected from the streets and sent to a centre specially established for them on the outskirts of the capital. The older boys and girls were recruited into a militia known as the Victory Pioneers, and were given full military training.

In the early days of the Revolution, to keep the people busy the Government introduced a programme called *Iskaa wax u qabso,* a sort of national self-help scheme. This programme involved construction of schools, hospitals and roads by the masses, under the supervision of the government-sponsored Orientation Centres, at the bidding of various Ministries and other government-controlled bodies.

The most disliked activity was the cleaning of the streets of Mogadishu, a recurring task which the citizens were called upon to do. Whenever the people moved from one side of the street to the other, the sand they had left behind in piles at the kerbside would be blown across the street again. We were being asked to clear the sand away from a desert. You cannot carry water in a sieve, but we were kept busy trying. This particular activity was called *Ol-olaha nadaafadda,* the cleaning campaign. On days when it was in operation, no civil servant was spared from becoming a street sweeper. Revolutionary activists from among the people would enter their houses and prise them out, if necessary. Oddly enough, the soldiers and militia did not participate in this campaign, but they came around to inspect the work, sitting atop their jeeps or landrovers. It was a cruel joke and demeaning for the senior civil servants, who had to bear the indignity. They were often the butt of insults from self-appointed revolutionaries, and often accused of sucking the blood of the people.

The members of the Supreme Revolutionary Council and members of the Government on the other hand, always came around with body-guards. They behaved like superstars. Everyone had to stand up for them and recite revolutionary songs in their honour.

The conditions in Somalia during this period resembled those which George Orwell had described in his famous book *Animal Farm*. So much so, in fact, that the Government had banned the circulation of *Animal Farm* in the country, and it was a crime to possess it. Someone was said to have translated the book into Somali, but for obvious reasons, that too had not seen the light of day in Somalia. Our system was a recognizable model of the Stalinist system. The use of terror against those who expressed dissent or who criticized the system was common practice. The word 'democratic' was applied in the most undemocratic way.

The socialist culture spread rapidly in the country. The President's status was raised by his Political Office to the level of the architects of international socialism—Marx, Engels and Lenin. The joint portraits of the latter were already displayed strategically in streets and on important buildings. To them was added a fourth face, that of the Founder of the Somali Revolution, the Father of the Somali Nation and the architect of Somali Scientific Socialism—Comrade Mohamed Siad Barre. It is interesting to recall that he also added his photograph to those of the thirteen members who had founded the SYL on 15 May 1943, though he was not one of them.

Whatever one's personal view of the President, he was undoubtedly a very strong character. When he addressed the people he had the knack of making his words stick in the minds of his audience. He could address and hold the attention of a mass rally for hours—a three-hour speech was not unusual—though he never took a written speech or notes with him to such gatherings. All his speeches were delivered impromptu. Although he wanted to implement a scientific socialism based on the ideas of Marxism-Leninism he quoted neither Marx nor Lenin. Moreover, he always used the Somali idiom and conventions of oratory.

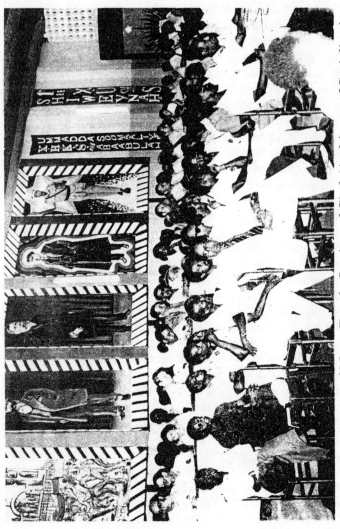

Life-size paintings of Marx, Engels, Lenin and Siad: 'Architects of Socialism'.

One of his most important achievements was the decision to adopt a script for the Somali language. On 21 October 1972, the President of the Supreme Revolutionary Council announced to the nation that the Revolutionary Government had chosen the Latin alphabet, with some modifications, as the official script for writing the Somali language.

During all of our history, the Somali language with its rich culture was never written. We spoke the language, we composed and recited poetry in the language, and we told stories in it, but we did not write it. During the nine years after independence, there were debates over selection of a script. While some interested parties wanted to adopt the Arabic script, others preferred Latin. A third script which was in existence was devised by a Somali, Osman Yusuf Kenadid, which had characters similar to Amharic and which was named Osmaniya, after its inventor. Before the Revolution, whenever the government of the day had raised the question of adopting a script for the language, different pressure groups would demonstrate against the move because it was known that the government—whichever government—favoured the adoption of Latin characters, for economic reasons as well as technical reasons, on the advice of trained Somali and international linguists. Osmaniya was impractical on several counts, besides having a distinct tribal association. The civilian governments in particular had been unable to resist the powerful pro-Arabic lobby, which would demonstrate outside the mosques after Friday prayers, whenever the issue was raised. They would chant slogans and carry banners about Latin being anti-Islamic.

The opponents of Latinization of the Somali language, however, did not dare raise their voices in protest when the Revolutionary Government announced its decision. Had they dared, they might have had to pay for it with their lives—as happened to some of their kind in a later incident during the Siad period. A month later, the Somali language was officially introduced in the administrative machinery of the government, replacing the two foreign languages which had hitherto prevailed. A campaign for learning the script was launched and an elaborate programme prepared to spread it throughout the whole territory. The slogan of the campaign was *'Haddaad taqaanno bar, haddaadan aqoonna baro'*, which meant 'if you know it teach it, if you do not know learn it'. Local radio broadcast programmes on reading and writing and teaching the language. The language programmes began with a wonderful song dedicated to the language:

Afkii qalaad ha moodin, carabku qaldi maayee, sidii caanaha qur-quriya.

Do not think it's a foreign language, the tongue will not miss it, drink it like milk.

In the Ministry of Foreign Affairs, too, we were instructed to send letters and notes to diplomatic missions in Somali, along with an unofficial translation in English or Italian or Arabic.

For financial and technical reasons, the language could not be developed overnight to the required level. Although it did not have the anticipated success, no one can deny that the decision to adopt a script for the language was a landmark achievement.

The Literacy Campaign was launched throughout the country and hundreds of intermediate and secondary school students and their teachers were sent to the interior, to teach villagers and nomads how to read and write. Besides this, the students and teachers were also given the tasks of enumerating the livestock population of the country and collecting folk literature from the various regions. It was the responsibility of each village and settlement to share the expense of accommodation and board of the literacy teachers for the period they stayed with the community.

Another programme introduced by the Revolutionary Government was the annual regional sports competition. Hundreds of young people, both boys and girls, gathered in the capital to compete in sporting events on behalf of their regions. While in the capital, the youngsters were accommodated by the inhabitants of Mogadishu, and treated not as guests but as family members.

At the opening ceremony of the sports competition each year, the President himself would address the participants, emphasizing the importance of sport in creating fraternity among the people of different regions. At these inauguration ceremonies, and at other public speaking engagements too, he always spoke about the fight against tribalism. He denounced tribalism but never seriously worked against it. In public, the President often thundered against the evils of tribalism but in the evenings he received tribal and clan leaders at the Presidency and discussed problems relating to their tribes with them. He knew very well how to deal with the Somalis, tribally and otherwise. He knew how to manipulate one clan against the other; to some he gave money, others were supplied with guns. On some he brought the full weight of the Government's displeasure to bear. To his own tribesmen he gave everything.

Part of my job was to arrange meetings and contacts between foreign diplomats and our leaders, including the President. Since we had declared ourselves socialists, the Soviet diplomats were more friendly towards us than the diplomats of some other countries, and accordingly, the Soviet diplomats received special attention and privileges. The Soviets were also involved in training the National Security Service people. A large number of Soviet experts also worked in the Ministry of Defence, since the country got most of its military equipment from the USSR.

One day, a Soviet military officer came to my office to obtain custom's clearance to import a duty-free car. The problem was that the car belonged to the Soviet Trade Office which had already used up its quota for importing duty free vehicles, so they were approaching us through Soviet experts in the Ministry of Defence, hoping and expecting that their clearance papers would get passed. The Soviet officer was in the company of a Somali military officer, presumably to convince us that the car was actually required for the Defence experts. After going through the papers, I told him that the Trade Office had already exhausted its quota for importing duty-free cars. The Russian officer was annoyed but went away.

A few days later I was called by the security people, who told me that I was endangering relations between the Soviet Union and Somalia. I knew the Russians would, if necessary, manage to get the papers cleared through the Ministry of Defence or the National Security Services. In both these organizations there were senior Soviet experts who would persuade the Somali authorities. I knew that I was playing with fire in turning down the Russian Trade Office request. The State Security could, if they so wished, interpret my behaviour as anti-revolutionary and finish me off in one of their dark rooms.

A Russian from the NSS finally did come to my office some days later to threaten me that I was obstructing the good relations between the two countries. But that was the last I heard of it.

Soviet help to Somalia was basically determined by the geo-strategic significance of our country in the context of superpower rivalry in world affairs. Their adversary, the United States, had very intimate relations with Ethiopia. Therefore, the Soviet Union needed Somali friendship to counter the growing influence of their rival in the Horn of Africa. Undoubtedly, Somalia also benefitted from its friendly relations with the USSR. Through this friendship we were helped to raise one of the most highly trained armies in Africa.

The Organization of African Unity Heads of State meeting was held in Mogadishu in 1974, When some of the African Heads of State who attended the OAU Summit were shown a display of military exercises, they could not believe that the pilots who were flying the planes in the air manoeuvres were Somalis. In order to convince them the President drove the guests to the airfield where the young pilots later landed. One of the visiting President remarked:

"Brother, you could single-handedly liberate South Africa." Some time later, the Somali Air Force not only trained pilots of Burundi, but also provided military experts, as well as nurses, to the fledgling state of Equatorial Guinea subsequent to its independence.

Other African Heads of State were more impressed by the way the Political Office worked, particularly its mass mobilization programme. It is true that the Office was able to organize large gatherings of the masses at very short notice. The African leaders were also impressed by how the people had been influenced apparently to love their leader. Interest in such aspects of Somali life by leaders who cherished dictatorial tendencies was borne out subsequently, when they sent groups of their countrymen for short training visits to Somalia.

The Zaire President, Mobuto Sese Seko had come to the Conference with a delegation of 110 members. Rumour was that he had brought all his opponents with him from both the military and civilian establishments, to prevent a coup against him during his absence from his country. Moreover, a Zairean airforce plane made two or three sorties every day, to keep him posted on all developments taking place in his country.

There was a wide difference between the statements delivered at the OAU Summit by some of the Heads of State and the actual relationship of their countries with the racist regime of South Africa, and with the Ian Smith regime of Rhodesia. Following Smith's Unilateral Declaration of Independence on 11 November 1965, the Africans decided to boycott all Rhodesian companies. OAU member states' views on this issue were unequivocal. And during the seventies, one of the member states actually forced the resignation of an OAU Secretary General for dealing with Lonrho (the London Rhodesia Company). Years later it was revealed that the same country which had accused the Secretary General had itself maintained very close cooperation with the same Lonrho Company up until 1980.

On the occasion of the OAU summit in Mogadishu, the Somali folklore group organized a theatrical programme. A pantomime scene portrayed the following as an example of how some States were actually behaving:

Scene: The Summit is about to commence. A white man is standing off to the side. He calls a member of an African delegation. The white man hands over to the black man, a brief-case, and makes signals suggesting that he disturb the meeting. A nodding African enters the hall. He takes the floor and speaks words to the effect that We Africans have no power, have no money, have no guns. We cannot do without the foreign powers

Next morning the head of delegation of one of the Southern African countries did not attend the meeting and, since I was Chief of Protocol, I had to go to the hotel where he was staying to enquire if there was anything I could do.

His Excellency was in his room. I told him, "Sir, the car is ready."

He replied: "I want to see the Minister of Foreign Affairs."

I could not imagine what was the matter. But I informed the Somali Minister of Foreign Affairs that he should come to the hotel.

"I am not going to the meeting today, and I protest against the show that your people presented last night," the foreign head of delegation told our minister. He had interpreted the sketch as a direct attack on his government. The necessary apologies and consolatory talk from the Somali Foreign Minister ultimately persuaded the delegate whose susceptibilities had been offended to attend the meeting.

This was the regrettable state of affairs in our part of the world. Some of us were really a bunch of hypocrites, paying lip service to the African causes, which were the agenda of the meeting. We Somalis had scrupulously implemented all the decisions taken by the OAU, and naively believed that other nations did the same. However, some African countries, particularly those who claimed to be in the vanguard of opposition to apartheid, maintained trade relations with the regime of South Africa throughout the period when the economic embargo was supposed to be enforced.

When a new building for the Ministry of Foreign Affairs was built, I was charged with allocating the rooms to various departments. I started by allocating the rooms on the floor meant for the Minister and the Director General. Of three adjacent rooms, the one on the right I allocated for the Minister's office and the one on the left for the Director General's. The remaining room between, I made a common reception room for both dignitaries. The architect had not planned for a separate sitting room for the Minister. The Minister's office was his only operational room, and there were always important papers on his desk. He could not clear his table every time someone arrived to visit him. This room, named the VIP room, would prevent that necessity, and it would be the responsibility of the Protocol to make sure the Minister's and DG's appointments did not clash.

I made similar arrangements for the rest of the Ministry. For the several Directors I allotted two meeting rooms on the ground floor for them to share. The Departments were arranged in accordance with the nature of their work, so that those with public dealings were allocated rooms on the ground floor and the Political and Economic Departments were accommodated on the first floor. The largest room on the first floor was assigned as a conference room.

After some time, the Minister decided he did not like the arrangement; he was especially unhappy with the separate reception rooms. He called a meeting of all the directors of the ministry. The directors expected that the minister wanted to discuss some political issue with them, or a new policy on the current world situation. They assembled in the conference room which was decorated with photographs of the President. From the huge hand-painted portrait on the wall behind the Minister to the smaller ones ranged around the room, it appeared as if the 'Father of Scientific Socialism' and 'Teacher of Marxism and Leninism' was observing the room from every angle. Wherever one looked one saw his face. The room presented an awful prospect to those who might have been ill-disposed towards the Revolution. They would surely suffer hallucinations, thinking perhaps that the portraits were rushing towards them, or blocking their passage out of the room! In such an atmosphere, all the officers of the Ministry gathered to hear the Minister's voice.

"Jaalleyaal," the Minister started his speech. "I have called the meeting this morning to tell you, since you are the most senior officials of the Ministry, that I trust you, and that the Revolutionary Government has trusted me to be your Minister. I say that you are all responsible persons and faithful to your country. From today, [it was some time in 1975] any one of you can receive any foreigner, diplomat or whomever else in your own office and not in the allotted reception rooms. The existing arrangement of separate VIP rooms in which to receive foreigners was the arrangement of Mohamed Osman who works with a communist mentality," he concluded.

It was true that this kind of arrangement existed in China, my previous posting. The strange thing, however, was that when I had been a student in Beijing as a young man years before, having had no previous association with the capitalist world, the verdict pronounced on me by my communist teachers had been 'a capitalist minded young man'. I can only say that I was and I continue a Somali.

It was ironic that a minister whose President preached the virtues of socialism and communism could pejoratively refer to someone as having a communist mentality. If the portraits could have heard what the Minister uttered, they would surely have moved in from the wall and battered him. If this was the way the Minister thought, it was his problem not mine. And, in those days, if one was called a communist it actually improved his career prospects.

In one of his speeches to the nation, President Siad had warned anti-revolutionaries that the Revolution had "ears and eyes everywhere". This proved to be true. Even before the directors had returned to their respective offices, an order came down from the President that whoever entertained a foreigner in his office would pay the price and that, whatever had been said to the contrary was null and void. I was on my way to my office on the ground floor when the news reached me. The furniture could hardly have been shifted from the VIP room, when the President's order was received in the Ministry!

Once, the Minister asked me to arrange a dinner for a particular Ambassador who was leaving the country after completing his tenure. Although the Minister had a good personal relationship with the Ambassador, the latter was reputed to have been engaged in activities detrimental to Somali national interests. Besides, the relations between his country and Somalia had really worsened during his tenure. So, what could be said in the farewell speeches at such a luncheon? I reminded the Minister of the problem, but he nevertheless confirmed the orders for the luncheon. I felt that this Ambassador, who had always stabbed us in the back, did not deserve to have money from the meagre budget of our poor country spent on him. The implication of holding such an occasions was that we appreciated the work of the guest of honour and were expressing our gratitude. The Minister and I were at one point alone in the room. I was annoyed, and said that if he wanted to give the dinner or lunch, he should ask the Administration to arrange it for him, and not me. Whether as a result of this incident, or because of some previously-held grudge, the Minister became less well-disposed towards me, and I soon found myself a pawn in the political battle which ensued in the Ministry.

The relations between the Minister and the Director General were tense. It was unfortunate that the two highest foreign policy planners of the country could not exchange views amicably, or evaluate together the contemporary international political situation. The differences between the two grandmasters had long divided the staff of the Ministry into two camps, one supporting the Minister and the other the Director General. Due to the nature of my duties, and the fact that I had to communicate personally with both on a daily basis, I had always avoided aligning myself with either group. I pretended to be unaware of what was going on around me.

The Director General was a powerful person, as he was a first cousin of the country's President. He was a very ambitious person. Somehow, he kept himself well-informed of the official goings on in the Ministry as well as the gossip in the corridors. I do not know whether somebody regularly briefed him, or if his knowledge was based on guesswork. He believed I was in the 'opposition camp'. Thus my position in the Ministry was as the proverb says, between the devil and the deep sea, or as the Italians say, '*Essere fra lincudine e il martello*'.

The time came when the Minister decided to remove me from the protocol office, and appointed me the director of administration. When the orders to this effect were issued, the Director General suspecting something fishy behind the transfer and an ulterior motive by the Minister, approached the President and had the transfer revoked. Some time later, the Minister appointed me Counsellor in the Somali Embassy in London. Everyone thought the Minister was doing me a favour, but in reality he only wanted to remove me from the Protocol. I, however, would have welcomed the transfer to London. It would have been my second opportunity to visit that beautiful and busy metropolis which had been my school of diplomatic training. But alas, again there was a Presidential decision to cancel my London posting.

I found myself between the two giants of the Ministry and became a victim of their conflict. I wanted to leave the country at all costs.

Protocol was a hectic job. In those years, the country's image in the world was soaring high. Many visitors came to the country. Besides organizing programmes for visitors from different countries, Protocol also dealt with the movements of foreign residents in the country, issued overflight and landing permission for aircraft, and was in charge of Public Relations. I was Chief of Protocol for six and a half years. During this period, I had no telephone facility at my house, which was somehow an advantage, for whenever my services were required a chauffeur driven car or a police patrol car came to fetch me. Had there been a telephone at my residence, the President's office, the Minister for Foreign Affairs, or any other leader would have just given orders by phone. It was also good for my personal security, for if they had to come and find me in the middle of the night, they also had to accompany me to wherever I was taken, which minimized the risk to my safety.

I was physically exhausted and was suffering from high blood pressure. The Chinese medical doctors had advised me to take leave from work to recuperate. An American doctor who used to visit the President had given me similar advice. However, I continued working.

Unlike in other communist countries, in Somalia we did not have sanatoriums for civil servants. What we had was the lunatic asylum or the security prison! Politicians and functionaries involved or accused of being involved in anti-revolutionary activities were usually sent to a prison located fifty kilometers away from the capital on the way to the city of Merca. None knew when one might be apprehended and sent to such a place.

While I was on a short leave from work, the Assistant deputed to Protocol in my absence was not sure what he should say to those who enquired about me. He knew I was on leave, but told people he did not know where I was. At a cocktail party at one of the embassies a few days after my return to work, a number of ambassadors and other diplomats remarked to me: "Are you still around?" They had interpreted my colleague's casual remark to mean I had been 'deposed', had disappeared in the manner familiar to most communist and totalitarian countries.

Of all the shocks I received, the most terrifying incident happened to me when a police patrol car came to my house one night and as usual knocked at the gate. I opened the door. I was wearing a *lunghi*—the relaxing and sleeping attire for Somali men. It was about 23:00 hours and I had been sleeping for about an hour. It was a Sunday night. They told me I was needed and to get dressed. I put on trousers and a shirt and went to the car, ready to go. The persons sitting in the car were unusually grim and serious that night.

The sergeant in charge spoke into the microphone of the radio,

"This is 27. This is 27. Can you hear me?"

"Very well," the other end said.

"We have the man. Where shall we take him?"

I was shocked because in the past they had always called me comrade, and spoken to me with respect. Now they referred to me as 'the man'. Something was seriously wrong. The thought occurred to me that this was to be my last night. I was taken to the police headquarters, and there I found also some people from the Somali Airlines and the Civil Aviation department whom I knew and who had been brought in for the same case—which was about to be revealed to us.

What had happened was that a Minister who was scheduled to fly abroad had arrived at the Airport that same afternoon without his passport. The passport was in my office, as the Minister had sent it to us to obtain the visa from the relevant embassy. We had got him the visa but no one had come to collect it. That afternoon the Minister had sent his driver to my house, and after together collecting the passport from my office, and for no particular reason, I went with him to the airport. By the time we reached there, the plane had already moved towards the runway and the Minister had missed his flight. As for me, it was not my duty to bring passports to the airport. His secretary or driver should have looked after those details.

During the ensuing investigation at the Police Headquarters, each of us was treated as if we had committed a crime of high treason.

"Why did you keep the passport of the Minister in your office?" was the first question.

"Because I was waiting for somebody to collect it."

"Why did you not send it to the Ministry?"

"That was not my duty, and I am not a messenger."

"Did you know the Minister was going to an important conference?"

"Yes. But the Minister was supposed to leave for the conference at a later date and not the one on which he went to the airport. We have a letter he sent us to confirm that. If he changed his mind, he could have sent someone to collect his passport on time."

The interrogation lasted hours, before they let us return to our houses, angry and nervous. During the Revolutionary regime it was a common practice to torture and terrorize innocent people. During investigations, people were stripped of rank and titles, and in our system, one was guilty until proven innocent.

The matter did not end here. Next morning, I received an urgent letter from one of the Vice-Presidents of the country, asking me to explain my position. I was surprised by the fact that the Vice-President of the country deemed it fit to intervene in such a matter, as if he had no other national problem to deal with. The letter's tone was that of an investigative questionnaire—after all this Vice President had been a police general! He and I knew each other personally, and I would have expected him to be on my side. I answered the letter with the same answers I had given during the police investigation. In addition I was able to attach documentary evidence of the Minister's intended date of departure.

The Minister did not succeed in making the passport episode a serious criminal case and it was, apparently, closed without further ado.

Another incident which has left a scar on my heart and hurt my feelings occurred in 1981 while I was in Rome with the President's delegation. One of the Presidential bodyguards punched me on my nose while I was on my way to the President's suite to brief him on the programme for the day. We were in Rome on a visit and the delegation stayed at the Hilton.

The incident happened—and until today I do not know why it happened—just in front of the President's suite and all the guards there witnessed it. I felt dizzy, but held myself from falling to the ground. I did not react, but returned to my room. I washed my face and came back to the President's suite.

"I have heard the news of the incident," said the President to me.

"Yes, Jaalle," I said, adding,

"I had been on my way to see you, as I do every day, and as is my duty."

The President said nothing, not even an apology which was too much to expect. He did not even sympathize with me. Besides, an apology was considered by some of us a sign of weakness. No action was taken against the bodyguard who punched me in the presence of at least ten people. And I was Chief of Protocol of the Republic! With all respect, the President could at least have ordered some sort of disciplinary action to be taken against the man who had physically attacked a high ranking official of the Ministry of Foreign Affairs, not for my sake but to uphold the dignity of my position. I knew those men would do anything to anyone and they were right all the time.

In truth, my country had been reduced to a police state. Anything could be manipulated, to be labelled ant-revolutionary. Even persons who had conceived and implemented the Revolution had long prison sentences imposed on them, while still others were sentenced to death and publicly executed for ant-revolutionary crimes. On April 20, 1970, General Jama Ali Korshel, First Vice-President of the SRC was arrested and charged with attempting to launch a *coup* with the assistance of a foreign power. A year later, General Mohamed Ainashe, Vice-President of the SRC, and General Salad Gavere, a senior SRC member and the Minister of Public Works, together with Major Abdulkadir Dhel, a former army officer, were executed by firing squad on July 23, 1972. Many believed that those who suffered imprisonment and death during the early stage of the Revolution had actually been the brains of the 'Blessed Revolution'. The ruling junta feared these revolutionaries and considered their survival a threat to their own grip on power. *

On 9 April, 1978, following the Ogaden war, some officers who were accused of attempting to overthrow the regime of Siad Barre were executed. Among the executed officers was Colonel Mohamed Sheikh Osman Irro who was said to have been the group leader.

Whenever the authorities were to executed a person at the police compound, Radio Mogadishu would play a particular song

* *A Government at War with its own People:* An Africa Watch Report; USA 1990

which was a sort of warning to the people to be careful in their behaviour and actions.

Same diidow	Those [of you] who
Dabin baa kuu dhigan	reject
Laguugu dili doonee	The goodwill [of the
Daneestow duulkaagu	Revolution]
Waa daldalaad	A trap awaits you;
Aan dacwo lahayn	You will be executed.
	Opportunists like you
	Face death by hanging,
	Without appeal

The song was also relayed on loudspeakers installed on mobile vans going around the city, with a view to terrorizing the people. The trial of such persons—those who were eventually executed by firing squad for treasonable offenses—was conducted by a special security court, not the regular judicial courts.

Somalia is among the 42 Least Developed Countries (LDCs) of the world, and among the ten poorest countries. On 14 February 1974, Somalia joined the League of Arab States which has some of the wealthiest countries among its members.

Had the oil-rich Arabs, our brothers, given us financial assistance to explore oil, it could have enabled us to wipe out our poverty and backwardness. For one reason or other, they preferred to bear the burden of our poverty instead. While not denying or under-estimating the massive assistance they generously gave us, it must be pointed out that Arab aid fell on stoney ground, in terms of benefit to the Somali people. Informally, however, our links with Arabia were a means of survival for many Somali families. Most of the Arab countries allowed Somali migrant workers into their countries, and the remittances they sent home were an economic lifeline for countless Somali families, and helped to create business opportunities for yet others.

CHAPTER IX

In Teheran

Until 1976, Somalia did not have a resident Mission in Iran. In June 1976, I was sent to Teheran as Charge d'Affaires to establish our embassy, pending the appointment of an ambassador.

The Government of Iran was showing deep sympathy and concern for our problems with our neighbours and the uneasy relations developing with the Soviet Union. The Iranian Foreign Minister, Abbas Ali Khaladbari had recently visited Somalia to express his country's support for us.

Since relations between Iran and the United States were very friendly then, and Iran sympathized with our problems, we presumed that Iranian overtures of support might have the approval of the Americans.

In the middle of the conflict in the Horn of Africa between Somalia and Ethiopia, in which Ethiopia was supported by the Soviet Union and its allies, I felt I should attempt to find out if the Americans actually were on our side.

I knew an American diplomat in Teheran. On several occasions we had exchanged ideas on the contemporary situation in Iran and its neighbouring countries. Our discussions had ranged widely, and we had talked about alleged human rights violations in Iran, the rumoured brutal activities of the SAVAK (the Security Service of Iran), and the activities of the opposition group against the regime of Shahan Shah Arya Mehr, Mohamed Reza Pahlavi.

One day I asked the American diplomat if he would enlighten me on the current US attitude towards the Ethiopians and their new found patrons, the Russians. I alluded to the fact that everything the Americans had invested in, in Ethiopia during their long links with that country, was now under the control of their adversary, the Soviet Union, and that since Somalia was currently at war with Ethiopia, and by extension with the Russians,

America might like to help Somalia with information regarding the location of important bases in that country.

As I expected, he told me he would see what he could do and, as I also expected, he did nothing. In our conflict with Ethiopia, the Americans could have been more helpful to us than any other country, but they always believed, no matter what happened, that the Ethiopians would, sooner or later return to their fold. They would not set fire to their own homes—they would not help us.

I was number two in our embassy, but knowing this did not help my American friend to learn what my precise duties were. In the embassies of the large and powerful countries, the secretaries—the First, Second and Third Secretaries—are usually believed to be from the secret services, the CIA, KGB, MI5 etc. In smaller embassies, like ours, everyone has to pitch in to fulfil all the tasks of the Mission including diplomatic, press, trade, and cultural, as well as gather information on matters of national interest.

Despite the enormous income from its oil revenues, the majority of Iran's population was extremely poor. In the southern part of the capital, the people lived in a very miserable condition. In some parts of the city, one could not drive a new car, certainly not a Mercedeze or a luxury car, for fear of being attacked by angry poor people. From time to time I went to Jaaleh Square, the capital's poorest area. I always parked my car at a distant place, and I never went there wearing a tie.

A large number of people in Iran lived simply on bread, cottage cheese and mint leaves. Only the upper class and middle class could afford good food at restaurants. The rich lived in the northern part of the city, which appeared a different world altogether. The Shah lived at his Niavaran Palace, apparently unconcerned or unaware of conditions in his country. Was it that those who surrounded him always informed him that the people were happy, that everything was going smoothly in the country, and that all was well with his *Takhte Taawoos*—his Peacock Throne?

The millions of dollars he got from oil exports were invested in armaments. The members of his family led a luxurious life. Their children were educated in Switzerland, and the masses were left to struggle for survival. In the rich neighbourhoods of the northern part of the capital, the wealthy class enjoyed an extravagant life. Dinner parties started with caviar and boiled Caspian Sea shrimps and ended with belly dancers.

Islam was supposed to be the religion of the country, in fact only the poorer section of the population had anything to do with religion. It was the poor who visited mosques to offer their prayers. Once, during the month of Ramadan, the Government of Iran organized an exhibition of old secret documents of the State. At the opening ceremony, which was presided over by a member of the Royal Family, drinks were served. This was in the morning, at about 10:00 o'clock. I expressed my surprise to the protocol officer, that food and drink were being served during the day in a Muslim country when the people were supposed to be fasting.

He reasoned that non-Muslims were also present. My contention was that the foreigners would not have expected to be served anything during the day in the month of Ramadan, and would respect our religious proscriptions. As a Muslim myself, I felt very strongly about this.

As ours was a small embassy, we employed only five local hands: a secretary, a typist cum telephone operator, a driver, a messenger and a watchman. As in many countries of the world, I knew that the local staff would either voluntarily go to the secret service to offer their services or otherwise the service agents would approach them as soon as it was known they were employed at an embassy.

The Iranian Secret Service, SAVAK, were in the habit of listening in to embassies' telephones. Sometimes, they would dial the embassies or the residences of diplomats, male and female, and mouth obscenities. This was extremely annoying and sometimes distressing. Yet, if the embassies reported this to the police, no action was ever taken to apprehend the delinquents.

I occupied some rooms on the top floor of the Chancery building. The flat below was occupied by the Secretary of the Embassy. One evening, when the telephone rang, I picked up the receiver—after office hours the telephone was connected to my apartment, and also had a parallel line to the room of the messenger. I heard the voice of the messenger who had picked up the receiver just before me. I kept silent and put my hand over the mouthpiece, so that he would not detect my breathing or the vacuum in the line.

The call was for him. The caller sounded authoritative. He told the messenger to come down to the petrol station that was situated at the end of our road. They spoke Persian and I understood the gist of their conversation. As soon as the receiver was put down I rushed to the balcony window of my flat, from where I could see the gates of the Chancery. I turned off the light before looking through a slit in the curtain, for he would have been able to see me had he looked up. The messenger came down to the gate, opened and shut it very quietly. I could see him clearly. He was in a great hurry, putting on his jacket while rushing to his rendezvous.

As soon as he moved out of sight I went out to the gate and locked it from the inside, so that the keys he had with him would not open it. I collected his clothes and belongings from his room and handed them to him when he returned. "You can come tomorrow morning for your wages," I told him, and did not allow him back on to the premises that night.

The messenger had been hired by us only recently, on the recommendation of a person we knew. His superiors should have waited a while, at least until he was well settled in the embassy, before trying to make use of his services.

At the embassy there were only three diplomats—the Ambassador, the Counsellor and a Second Secretary. Every Tuesday morning, before we began work, the Ambassador gathered us in his office and lectured us on the virtues of socialism and the 'Blessed Revolution'. About the President of the Supreme Revolutionary Council, Mohamed Siad Barre, he would tell us that The Father of the Somali Nation had dedicated his life to the people.

At the end of these weekly meetings we would pledge to follow the commandments of the Political Office, and we would stand and sing *Guul Wade Siad,* the song dedicated to the President. This behaviour was bizarre, and we appeared stupid, but we had no choice in the matter. None of us dared to question our actions. I would have liked to know, how serious the Ambassador was about this veneration, but could not ask. The local staff, sitting in adjacent rooms, could hear us singing. They too must have wondered what we were doing, but would not dare ask. For anyone to raise questions would have been criticism of the Revolution, and considered *kacaan diid.*

Despite the little irritations that the Secret Service caused the diplomatic missions, including ours, relations between Somalia and Iran were very good, and the Iranian Government gave strong moral support to the Somali cause.

In the midst of the high tension in the Horn of Africa, where the struggle for the liberation of the Ogaden had escalated into war between the Somalis and Ethiopians, the President of the United States of America, Jimmy Carter came on an official visit to Iran

A formidable section of the Western media was on our side just then. Since the media in the West has a reputation for influencing public opinion, as well as moulding the minds of their leaders, we thought President Carter should have some sympathy for the Somali position. Moreover, since the Horn of Africa was a current flashpoint in world events, it must have been on the agenda for his discussions with the Iranian Monarch.

Soon after President Carter had left Teheran, one of the Iranian national dailies carried a report titled: 'Whoever harms Somalia will be considered as harming Iran'. In other words Somalia's enemy was the enemy of Iran. We were very happy at this turn of events as it seemed that President Carter and the Shah of Iran had indeed discussed our problems during their meeting, and agreed to support Somalia. I could not persuade myself to believe that the press report was a mere coincidence, as in those days the press in Iran was tightly controlled and could not publish anything that did not have the Government's blessing. Added to which, the Government of Iran always consulted their US friends before taking any initiative in foreign affairs.

A few days later, a high ranking Iranian Army Officer confided to us in the embassy that Iran was indeed preparing to send some assistance to Somalia. He also implied that Iran was waiting for approval from the White House for the assistance to be airlifted to Mogadishu.

The Ethiopians were already receiving all kinds of support from the Russians and the Cubans. According to our information, military experts and intelligence officers from Eastern Europe were also working as advisors in Ethiopia. There were reports that pilots from South Yemen were assisting the Ethiopian Air Force in its bombardment of Somalia.

The Iranian Officer was to keep in touch with me. Several days passed, and I began getting a little anxious about the delay. If they, USA and Iran, had agreed to help us, what was taking so long? Our expectations had been raised by the Iranian promise of assistance, following the US President's visit. We could not imagine that there would be any hold ups.

Yet, all our hopes and expectations were dashed to the ground when the American Ambassador to Iran, Mr. Sullivan informed us that the White House had objected to the Iranian offer of assistance. For a moment we were stunned by the statement of the US Ambassador. We did not react. It was not for us to ask why. The USA did what it considered best for its own national interests. But, keeping in mind the fact that Somalia was fighting the Ethiopians, who had embraced communism, and that the new communist regime there had expelled all Americans from its soil, and that the Russians and their allies—all enemies of the United States and the West—were openly supporting Ethiopia, we were unable to understand the negative response of the Americans. Somalia had freed itself from Soviet influence, and the US could have filled the vacuum and re-established its influence in the region.

Due to Somalia's refusal to accept Soviet and Cuban mediatory efforts to resolve our dispute with Ethiopia, and due to the creation of a regional alliance between Ethiopia, Somalia and South Yemen under the USSR's patronage, the entire Eastern bloc had turned hostile to us. Ultimately this led to escalation of the conflict in the Horn of Africa. Had we accepted their 'peace proposals' it would have opened the flood gate for Russian domination of the entire region.

The war was going very well for Somalia, in any case. Somali soldiers had captured a large number of sophisticated weapons from the Ethiopians, who were abandoning the sites they were supposed to defend. However, the Somali forces needed continued supplies of arms and ammunition to retain their gains, and stockpiles of armaments in the country were fast depleting.

The US Administration was unwilling to accept that the Ogaden was part of Somalia. In 1946, the USA and the Soviets had opposed the British proposal that all the Somali territories be brought together. And when, at a later date, the British gave the Ogaden to the Ethiopians, both superpowers remained silent. Again in 1977, the USA and the USSR in their different ways opposed the liberation of the Ogaden—the Russians by directly fighting against Somalis, and the Americans by opposing Iran's proposed assistance to Somalia.

From Iran, I was transferred to our embassy in Dar-es-Salaam, Tanzania. Before proceeding to the new posting I went home for a short vacation.

At the Ministry I met with the Director General for consultations about my past and my future posting. He told me that the Iranians had accused me of being a Russian spy. The Iranians had accused me of this in a letter sent through their embassy in Mogadishu. The Director General, the senior most officer after the Minister, also informed me that the Ministry was of the opinion that the allegation was in reaction to what I had been reporting about the authorities, the system, the opposition, and the Secret Service in Iran, and therefore, he said "we believe that they must have been opening our diplomatic pouch before passing it to the airlines."

I did not see the Iranian letter. However, whatever they said about me, I believe it was a very inept attempt at creating a misunderstanding between a diplomat and his government. If they had alleged that I was a close friend of the Americans that might have carried some weight, because the Secret Service noted my having lunch or dinner with my American acquaintance, even though they would not have known the substance of our conversation. On the other hand, I could not even remember saying more than a 'hello' to a Russian while I was in Iran. The same subject was also mentioned to me by the President when I visited him.

Regarding the possibility of opening of diplomatic bags, this could easily have been accomplished. Our embassy normally sent its mail via the cargo section of Iran Air. As it was a simple pouch it was possible to open it and each of the envelopes in it, photocopy and re-seal them and then close the pouch again. Like Somali Embassies elsewhere, our embassy in Teheran purchased all requirements in the local market, including the wax, rubber stamps, and the envelopes. Iran Air, moreover, compelled us to deliver our mail to them well in advance of the flight, which would give them ample time to tamper with the pouch if they wanted. The Iranians were very sensitive about any criticism of their system, particularly regarding the Shah and SAVAK.

I had noticed something very similar when I was in China in 1971, when our pouch came from Mogadishu via Moscow and Irkutski in the USSR. I had the feeling the Soviets were opening it before sending it to Beijing, as it was always unnecessarily delayed on the way. I had made a written observation on this to our Ministry, and had suggested ways to improve the Dipmail, even though sending the pouch by courier to each country where we had our embassies was economically impossible for us.

When I was told about the Iranian allegation against me, I was not at all surprised. Like Iran, Somalia was ruled by a dictatorial regime, and they had expected I would be punished in the same way that their own dictator dealt with his people. But this time the revolutionary government was on my side.

Throughout the period when I was in Iran, Shah Mohamed Reza Pahlavi's regime was torturing and killing innocent people. Had the Shah utilized national resources for the common good, with the oil revenues of a single month, he could have built an apartment for each of his 35 million citizens. Yet, the majority of his people neither had adequate nourishment nor a place of shelter. Anyone who visited Jaaleh Square in Teheran could foresee the impending doom of the Shah's regime. The tolerance of the common people suffering abject poverty on the one hand, against the glittering lifestyle of the rich was bound to reach bursting point.

The Shah's advisors who presented a rosy picture of the dismal conditions of his people were his real enemies. But so too were his foreign friends (or masters) who considered themselves champions of human rights. They never gave him sincere advice, much less condemn the rampant violations of basic and fundamental rights to life and existence.

The Shah himself never thought that the wealth he had accumulated belonged to the people. Instead, he deposited hundreds of millions of dollars in US banks. It was surely some kind of poetic justice when he was refused entry to that country after he was compelled to flee his homeland in the wake of the popular Islamic revolution of Khomeini. His friends denied him the opportunity to spend his last days in peace in their midst, or even a place to die. He followed his own father's destiny, who had died in an asylum and was buried in South Africa. Thanks to the late Egyptian President Anwar Sadat, the Shah was allowed to land in Cairo and at his death to be buried there.

During my stay in Teheran, I was privileged to enjoy the friendship of many common people. I visited their homes and they also came to see me at my place. These Iranian friends would frequently tell me that a man at the gate had tried to stop them entering, or had asked them their names. I had no guard at the gate, and I worried for their safety.

In spite of the seemingly watertight power of the Government, the Opposition was very strong in Teheran. This was reflected in the fact that there were open attacks from time to time against foreigners of countries that supported the Shah's regime, and the Ambassador of a country which was a powerful ally of the Shah did not dare fly the national flag on his car, but preferred to travel incognito. He was protected by armed guards and sharp-shooters. This Ambassador drove to cocktails with two or three similar cars as cover, so that it was not known in which car he was travelling.

The Government called the opposition who were operating within the country, Islamic Marxists.

CHAPTER X

The Growing Rift between Somalia and its Socialist Allies

In 1974 the King of Kings, the Lion of Judah, Emperor Haile Selassie was overthrown in a military coup by Colonel Mengistu Haile Mariam. Colonel Mengistu took charge and appointed himself Chairman of the Provisional Government of Ethiopia. He also declared the adoption of a system of Socialism by the country.

These sudden changes in Ethiopia were a great setback for the Western powers who had been its generous patron throughout Ethiopia's existence, and had influenced its domestic and external policies. For us, Ethiopia's long-standing adversary, it made no difference, so long as the new regime did not allow the people of the Ogaden to exercise their right to national self-determination.

As the self-proclaimed defender of European interests in the region, Ethiopia had attracted the sympathy of the Christian world. The Emperor had once described Ethiopia as 'a Christian island in a sea of pagans'. Now, suddenly, it had changed its colours and started to propagate the theory that religion is the opium of the toiling masses.

The Soviet Union welcomed the changes in Ethiopia as a positive development, so far as their interests in the region were concerned. Somalia and South Yemen were already under Soviet influence. Now with Ethiopia joining the group, the Soviets would be able to substantially tighten their control over the Indian Ocean and the Red Sea. A look at the map shows that Somalia forms the north-eastern tip of Africa, where it juts out into the Indian Ocean, and its 3200 kilometers of coastline runs from the Bab-el-Mandeb, known as the southern gate of the Red Sea, eastward along the Gulf of Aden to Cape Guardafui, and south-westward along the Indian Ocean to Ras Kiamboni at the border with Kenya. South Yemen had the strategic port of Aden, at the confluence of the Indian Ocean and the Red Sea's Gulf of Aden.

In May 1977, the Russians organized a summit meeting in Aden between Somalia, Ethiopia and the People's Democratic Republic of Yemen (PDRY) in order to consolidate their strategic gains in this region. The overtly stated objective of the meeting was to cultivate understanding among the leaders of socialist countries. The meeting was attended by the top rank leadership of the three countries—Abdul Fattah Ismail, Secretary General of the Socialist Party of PDRY and Salim Rubaia Ali, Head of the Presidential Council of PDRY; President Siad Barre for Somalia; and Colonel Mengistu for Ethiopia, as well as Fidel Castro of Cuba. The Soviets made brave efforts to foster fraternal feelings among these leaders who had embraced socialism, but the meeting came to grief when Somalia and Ethiopia deadlocked over the Ogaden. The Somalis could not easily sacrifice the interests of their brothers in the Ogaden, and any understanding or compromise which did not include freedom of Western Somalia was not acceptable to us. The Ethiopians, for their part, wanted an agreement which did not concede the right of self-determination to the Ogaden people.

It was clearly in the Russian interest to make every effort to persuade the intransigent Somalis to come to an understanding with Ethiopia. President Podgorny visited Somalia in March 1977 to discuss this objective with the Somali leaders. Siad Barre, however, refused to entertain any proposal which did not include the right to self-determination for the Ogaden. Then President Fidel Castro of Cuba came to Somalia with the same objective. Again Somalia rejected the proposal. At a public meeting in Mogadishu, Fidel Castro was outspoken in his criticism of his hosts, and in contrast showered praise on Mengistu.

The Russians and the Cubans believed that the aid and assistance they gave to Somalia could enable them to put sufficient pressure on our country to bend to their will. They misjudged the historical significance of Somali-Ethiopian animosity and the depth of the feeling which Somalis had for the territories in question. They did not realize that Somalia could not be forced to abandon what it considered to be its national interests.

As the conflict between Somalia and the Soviet Union

deepened, the Somali Government accused the Soviet Union of providing Ethiopia with huge military support and Cuba for providing combat troops and other military personnel. It was said that there were 17,000-19,000 Cubans in Western Somalia and elsewhere. It was time to send the Soviets packing from Somalia.

On 18 November 1977, the Somali Permanent Mission at the United Nations issued a Press Release to the world on Somali/Soviet relations. It stated:

> '...The Soviet Union had unilaterally violated the letter and spirit of the Treaty of Friendship and Cooperation of 11 July, 1977. The Somali Government had no choice but to declare the Treaty invalid; revoke the land and naval facilities accorded to the Soviet Union; ask all Soviet military experts or civilian technical staff to leave the Somali Democratic Republic within 7 days with effect from 13/11/77; ask for a mutual reduction of embassy staffs in Modagiscio and Moscow and to sever diplomatic relations with Cuba.'

This was a severe set-back to the Soviet Union, but it was a great joy for the Somalis. It was celebrated like a second independence day in Mogadishu. A large number of people came out on the streets with green leaves to welcome the decision of the Government. The spontaneity of the demonstration was in marked contrast to the staged rallies which had been the order of the day for some years past. The President reportedly commented: "It seems it was only I who was keeping the Russians here."

The Soviet Military contingent expelled from Somalia was despatched to Ethiopia to take up anti-Somali duties there.

The Russians increased the deployment of personnel from their satellite countries. There were rumours saying that Cuban soldiers also were flown in from Angola to Ethiopia, via Kilimanjaro airport in Tanzania. The flights that were bringing the Cuban troops from Angola were making a stopover at that regional airport of Tanzania, a country which for some time past had been preaching peace, unity and stability in Africa!

The ruling élite of Tanzania enjoyed the patronage and sympathies of the Christian world. Its supreme leader, Julius Nyerere opposed the independence of Western Somalia. Although he projected himself as a great champion of African unity, he was rumoured to have encouraged the separatists in the Shaba Province of Zaire and allegedly allowed them to launch the attack on Shaba from his own country. This champion of African unity, who refused to recognize the right to self-determination for the Ogaden Somalis, on the pretext of supporting Ethiopia's territorial integrity, was also among a handful of African countries to offer recognition to the breakaway Nigerian region of Biafra. Nyerere was never a friend of Somalia.

The relations between Somalia and Tanzania were very bad. We in the embassy were denied easy access to their Foreign Ministry although one high ranking official had been a fellow diplomat with me in China in the 1970s. Tanzania's support for Ethiopia's colonization of the Somali territory of the Ogaden, made our position as diplomats in Dar-es-Salaam very difficult, similar to the Soviets' position in Beijing when relations between those two countries were at their lowest ebb.

On one of the few occasion when I had the opportunity to meet a Tanzania Foreign Ministry official, although he was unwilling to discuss our bilateral relations, we did manage to talk about Zambia, which was then facing a severe drought and shortage of their staple food. I expressed my apprehensions that if the Tanzanian government did not do everything possible to reduce the reputed long hold-ups of Zambian cargo at the port and expedite the clearance of foodstuffs destined for that country, Zambia might open its border with the rebel regime of Ian Smith to get the desperately-needed food for his people.

My Tanzanian friend informed me that he believed that so long as President Kenneth Kaunda was Head of State, he would abide by the decision of the Organization of African Unity and Zambia would not break the sanctions. My view was that if faced with the choice, President Kaunda would prefer to save the lives of his people, and that decision hung on Tanzania facilitating the clearance of foodstuffs from their port. Zambia might otherwise be compelled to break the sanctions and open the southern trading route.

As it happened, a few months later, Zambia decided to open the southern route to import the necessary grain. Before doing so, Kaunda sent an emissary to Nyerere to brief him on the situation. Nyerere was reportedly furious and tried to dissuade

Zambia from breaking the sanctions. But what was truly amazing about President Nyerere was his desire that others not break the OAU resolution on Rhodesia when he was violating the sanctions himself. Tanzania had economic relations with the Lonrho Company, and allowed its factories to continue functioning on its territory. Ethiopia has no sea ports and is a land-locked country. Due to the continuous fighting by the Eritereans in their struggle for liberation, Ethiopia found it very difficult to maintain normal functioning of the Eritrean Red Sea ports.

Often, it had to depend on the port of Djibouti for handling supplies of essential goods from outside and the export of its goods to the world. It had always been said that Emperor Haile Selassie was in favour of France continuing its stay in the territory, so that the flow of their goods and the running of what they called the vital Djibouti-Addis railway, would continue unhindered.

The Abyssinians were afraid that if Djibouti became free and joined with the rest of independent Somalia whose relations with Ethiopia were not cordial, their national interests would be jeopardized. It was said to be one of the conditions, agreed to by Siad Barre, that Djibouti was granted independence on 27 June 1977, provided it would stay a separate Republic and not unite with Somalia—this in order to satisfy the Ethiopians.

In the past, the USA had given massive assistance to Ethiopia which in turn had granted it facilities for building military and communication bases in the country. In Somalia, the Russians had been similarly allowed to develop and use port facilities at Berbera.

Following the overthrow of Haile Selassie, who had long been a trusted ally of the West, the new 'Red Emperor' of Ethiopia, Mengistu switched his country's allegiance to the Soviet Union. Somalia had felt that the USA would come to its assistance as a consequence, but this did not happen. This was a great disappointment to the Somalis, who felt that, due to its geostrategic significance on the Horn of Africa, its long coastline, and its secure ports, it should have been coveted by either of the superpowers. It was felt that the Americans would move to our support with massive aid. When this did not happen, we came to the conclusion that America must still hope to win Ethiopia back, and would meanwhile not allow Somalia to become strong enough to pose any future threat to the Ethiopians.

I arrived in Dar-es-Salaam at the beginning of 1978. As the Liberation Committee of the Organization of African Unity had its headquarters in Dar-es-Salaam, a number of African Liberation movements had also established their offices there. Some of the prominent movements active in Dar-es-Salaam were ZANU/ZAPU PF, the liberation movement against the illegal Rhodesian regime, the ANC and PAC movements against the apartheid and minority regime in South Africa, and SWAPO, the movement for the liberation of Namibia. ·

At meetings of the Liberation Committee, member state representatives always spoke eloquently against regimes under which the black peoples were oppressed and suppressed. They delivered speeches full of emotion on the need to liberate black people from the clutches of the racists. We advocated the economic boycott of the two regimes in southern Africa.

However, the deeds of some members of the OAU, who were also members of the Liberation Committee, were rather different from the speeches they used to deliver. For example, not all member countries followed the OAU decisions relating to the boycotts. And, just as some of these countries had secret dealings with the two regimes in question, some leaders of liberation struggles bought themselves cars made in South Africa, from funds supplied to them by the OAU.

The common people were laying down their lives for their countries, while their leaders were often cooperating with the enemies of these African freedom fighters. The liberation of Africa became possible not because some leaders spoke for it at international forums, but because the people fought for it, and blood was spilt. In the end, everyone has to live with his own conscience, and that goes also for the politicians and national leaders who spoke for their 'beloved continent' or 'beloved country', and did quite the contrary.

CHAPTER XI

The Gap between Saying and Doing

After four years of absence from home, I returned to Mogadishu in January 1980 and was re-appointed Chief of Protocol at the Ministry of Foreign Affairs—the post I had held from 1972 to 1976.

The country was in the eleventh year of the Revolution. We had started out on 21 October 1969 with great enthusiasm and hope, but ten years later we were in a state of despair. During this period, we had lost a war with the Russian-backed forces of Ethiopia. How many Somalis had been killed in the war we never learnt.

Although most Somalis had suffered the agony of losing a friend or a relative in the war, no one blamed the President for pitting the country's strength against Ethiopia for the liberation of the Ogaden. Everyone still felt that the liberation of the occupied territories was a legitimate cause and every Somali was prepared to offer any sacrifice for its achievement. In this, the President had the complete support and trust of the people.

Thousands of war disabled were brought to the capital's hospitals. Some, fortunate to have a tribal connection with the leadership, were sent abroad for treatment at State expense while 'the others' were dumped in De Martini Hospital, where it soon became apparent that provision was not being made for their proper treatment. On several occasions, the crippled servicemen sent representation to the Minister of Defence, complaining about the poor treatment and lack of care in the hospital.

The De Martini hospital had, in fact, been abandoned a long time before. It was dilapidated and lacked proper repair and maintenance. The window-bars had rusted and the roofs of most of the wards had fallen in. Though the Government had partially repaired the hospital, it was still an unfit place for sick people.

The Government's behaviour could be compared to the owner

of a horse who had used the animal until it could work no more and then, when it became sick, he shot it dead. The crippled and injured servicemen were not shot, they were ignored by the government. Certain foreign non-governmental voluntary organizations did sometimes provide some medical treatment, but it was totally inadequate.

In the post-war period opposition groups, some operating underground, others from abroad, began agitating against the President and his regime. The Army was deployed to suppress these agitators, and to search and destroy the opposition operating along the borders. The National Security Service and the National Security Court increased their activities.

By now, it was widely held that it would have been better had President Siad relinquished power and let the people choose new representatives by election. Even those who blamed him for mismanagement of the country's affairs would probably have forgiven him if he had made the gesture to stand down. His popularity had been high among the masses during the early heady years of the Revolution. Had he conceded to hold elections for a parliament based on a multi-party system, there was a fair chance he might have been elected with a thumping majority, thus legitimizing his authority.

Or if he had just left the throne, telling the people, "I have done what I could do. I wanted to liberate the Ogaden, and failed. I have adopted a script for the Somali language, I have done this and that..." he may have carried the day. Perhaps, the people would have hailed him as a hero, and demanded that he stay. But Siad decided to handle affairs differently.

Siad had formed the Somali Revolutionary Socialist Party in July 1976, appointed himself as its Secretary General and offered himself as the sole candidate for the post of President, reducing the country to a one-man dictatorship. Accordingly, the Chairman of the Supreme Revolutionary Council, SRC, had issued Charter Three of the Revolution which, among other things, stated:

'Art. 1 : With effect from 1st July 1976 a national political party called Somali Revolutionary Socialist Party has been established;

'Art. 3 : The Somali Revolutionary Socialist Party is the only

Third Charter of the Revolution.

JAMHUURIYADDA DIMUQRAADIGA SOOMAALIYA

MADAXTOOYADA GOLAHA SARE EE KACAANKA

XAASHIDII SADDEXAAD EE KACAANKA

GUDDOONSHAHA

GOLAHA SARE EE KACAANKA

ISAGOO ARKAY : Xaashidii Koowaad iyo tii Labaad ee Kacaanka iyo Sharcigii 1aad ee soo baxay 21kii Oktoobar 1969;

ISAGOO ARKAY : Horukaca ay Ummadda Soomaaliyeed gaartay dhinaca Siyaasadda, Dhaqaalaha iyo Bulshada ka dib intii uu jiray Kacaanka Oktoobar;

ISAGOO TIXGELIYEY: Guulaha waaweyn ee uu xaqiijiyey Kacaanka Oktoobar iyo hirgelinta mabaadi'da caddaaladda, sinnaanta iyo midnimada iyo biseylka garaadka siyaasiga ah ay Ummadda Soomaaliyeed gaartay;

ISAGOO AQOONSADAY: Inay Ummadda Soomaaliyeed hadda diyaar u tahay inay si toos ah uga qayb qaadato siyaasadda iyo Maamulka Guud ee Dalka, sidaas darteedna loo baahan yahay in la abuuro Xisbi Hantiwadaag ah oo salka ku haya mabaadi'da iyo himilooyinka Kacaanka Oktoobar;

ISAGOO FULINAAYA: Mabaadi'dii iyo ujeeddooyinkii lagu caddeeyey Xaashida Koowaad iyo tan Labaad ee Kacaanka;

ISAGOO TIXGELIYEY: Go'aankii ka soo baxay Golaha Sare ee Kacaanka fadhigiisii 8da Juunyo 1976;

WUXUU GUDDOOMIYEY

1. Marka laga billaabo 1da Luulyo 1976 waxaa la dhisay Xisbi Siyaasi ah ee waddani ah laguna magacaabo Xisbiga HANTIWADAAGGA EE KACAANKA SOOMAALIYEED.

2. Xisbigu wuxuu lahaan doonaa astaan iyo jiritaan sharci ah.

3. Xisbiga Hantiwadaagga ee Kacaanka Soomaaliyeed waa midka qura ee ka jiri kara Dalka Jamhuuriyadda Dimuqraadiga ee Soomaaliya, lamana abuuri karo Xisbi kale ama urur siyaasi ah oo aan ahayn midka ku xusan Qodobka 1aad ee Guddoonkan.

4. Xisbiga Xaruntiisu waxay noqonaysaa Xamar, wuxuuna ku yeelan karaa laamo iyo xubno Gobollada, Degmooyinka, Tuullooyinka, Wasaaradaha, Wakaaladaha, Warshadaha, Xarumaha Ciidammada Qalabka Sida iyo hadba meeshii kale ee looga baahdo.

5. Calaamadda Xisbiga waa BURRUS iyo YAAMBO isdhaafsan oo XIDDIGTA Calanka Soomaaliyeed kor ka saaran tahay iyo labo CALEEMOOD oo ku wareegsan.

6. Xisbigu wuxuu sii wadaysaa Mabaadi'dii iyo Siyaasaddii Kacaanka ee ku caddeyd Xaashida Koowaad iyo tan Labaad ee Kacaanka Oktoobar; ujeeddadiisuna waa hirgelinta Mabda'a Hantiwadaagga Cilmiga ku dhisan ee ku cad Xaashida Labaad ee Kacaanka.

7. Xisbigu wuxuu yeelan doonaa destuur u gaar ah iyo xeer hoose oo saameeya qaabka iyo habka maamulka Xisbiga.

8. Marka laga billaabo Kowda Luulyo 1976, Golaha Sare ee Kacaanku, xukunkii iyo awooddii maamulka Dalka ee uu kula wareegay Sharciga 1ambarkiisu yahay 1 (kow) ee soo baxay 21kii Oktoobar 1969, wuxuu ku wareejiyay Xisbiga Hantiwadaagga ee Kacaanka Soomaaliyeed - Golaheeda Siyaasiga ah.

9. Muddo shan sano gudasheed, haddii aanay imaan dhibaato laga fursan waayay, waa in la soo saaro Dastuurkii lagu maamulayey Dalka.

10. Muddada ku meel gaarka ah, ka hor intaan la soo saarin Dastuurka Dalka, awoodda sharci dejinta Dalka waxay Guddiga Dhexe ee Xisbigu u xitsaari doontaa Guddi gaar ah oo uu Guddoomiye ka yahay Xoghayaha Guud ee Xisbiga ama cid ka wakiil ah.

11. Xubnaha Guddiga kor ku xusan iyo habka uu ku shaqayn doono waxaa lagu soo saari doonaa xeer u gaar ah.

12. Guddoonkaani wuxuu dhaqan galayaa marka uu saxiixo Madaxweynaha Golaha Sare ee Kacaanka, waxaana lagu soo saari doonaa Faafinta Rasmiga ee Jamhuuriyadda Dimuqraadiga ee Soomaaliya.

Muqdisho. 1 Luulyo 1976.

(Sarreeye Gaas Maxamed Siyaad Barre)
Madaxweynaha G. S. K.

party that exists in the Somali Democratic Republic and no other
Party or political organization which is not the one mentioned in
Art. 1 of this Charter is allowed.'

Along with giving himself sweeping powers, Siad Barre was
decreeing the foundation day of his party to be the 1st of July, the
day which had hithertoo been celebrated as our Independence
Day. Apparently he intended to abolish the imp ortance of that
event, and substitute it with a piece of his own history. Already
he had changed our national day celebrations from July 1st to
October 21st. Soon he would take the 15th May, which from the
1940s had been marked as the founding day of the Somali Youth
League, and change it to Youth Day. Siad was comandeering all
of our history and substituting his own.

As opposition to his regime grew over the years, Siad Barre
sought to suppress it with an iron hand.

There was great frustration among the intellectuals. While
the illiterate, ignorant and inexperienced—but with certain
tribal connections—or those with a party apparatchik background, enjoyed the patronage of the regime, were appointed to
important positions in the Government machinery and wielded
great power and influence, while intellectuals were kept under
surveillance.

In earlier days, the Ministry of Foreign Affairs was one of the
most prestigious places to work. Young men and women from different social backgrounds joined the Ministry after undergoing
training at the Halane training camp. As in other ministries and
government departments, the working conditions in the Ministry of Foreign Affairs were relatively good during the early years
of the Revolution. And, even though members of certain
privileged tribes were appointed as ambassadors and diplomats,
the interests of other tribes were also taken into consideration.

The Foreign Ministry did not apply a Foreign Service Law,
neither did it have rules, procedures and norms for posting of officials to Somali Diplomatic Missions abroad. The Minister enjoyed almost unfettered power and privilege in assigning
officials to whatever posting he deemed them competent for.
Once, when the Minister was asked why the Ministry did not
post staff according to a set of foreign service rules and proce-

dures, he replied that if everyone knew when and where he was to go abroad, what was the Minister to occupy himself with.

The result of such *ad hoc* functioning was that the Ministry became the property of privileged persons. The children of influential people, or the relatives of influential people, who were recommended for foreign service posts did not work at the Ministry for even a short period to try and learn something before being posted abroad. Some of the President's nominees did not even know the location of the Ministry until it was time to collect their diplomatic passports and tickets. Others, perhaps children of the new elite, and already benefitting from state scholarships to foreign universities, were directly absorbed into the Somali Embassy of the country where they were living, without even returning home first.

Due to inflation, life in the capital had become very difficult, particularly for those with fixed incomes. Civil servants especially, for whom there were no financial incentives or a progressive salary structure, found it difficult to manage a decent life. Standard rates of pay in the civil service had remained static and only covered one or two weeks needs. Consequently, absenteeism in the offices increased. Some officials showed up in the morning to sign the attendance register and left. They went downtown in search of part-time work or business, to make a little more money.

At the beginning of the Revolution in 1969, most people enjoyed a more or less equal standard of living with the exception of those who had used their positions to enrich themselves by misappropriating State properties, and this embezzlement had not been on a large scale.

The feelings of uncertainty and insecurity were growing among the ruling elite. Both in the capital and outside, opposition activity was on the rise. The promises of the Revolutionary Government to fight against widespread injustice, profiteering and embezzlement of public funds had lost their credibility. The declarations on restoration of justice, equality before the law of the land, the right to work, the people's right to run their own affairs, fair distribution of the nation's income, eradication of hunger, disease and ignorance, and the elimination of the insidious system of tribalism, all sounded very hollow and were violated with impunity.

Contrary to the declarations and promises of the Revolutionary Council there was rampant corruption, and widespread injustice and violation of human rights which the judicial system failed to address. In the courts, only those who had power or money won their cases. The National Security Court had the power to arrest people and keep them in the dark hole *Godka* without trial for as long as the regime desired.

Many who were allegedly involved in anti-revolutionary activities or suspected of conspiring to stage coups against the Revolutionary regime were sentenced to death by the National Security Court. The Court could never bring those to book who were actually turning the country bankrupt; for propaganda purposes, they handed down death sentences or life imprisonment to others who had allegedly misappropriated public funds, even though these 'criminals' were probably only petty thieves.

Contrary to what the Revolution had promised, the embezzlement of public funds became a regular feature. Many of those employed to manage the assistance given by international organizations for development projects embezzled the funds with the knowledge of influential leaders. Some were even allowed to choose the institution in which they wished to work. Certain appointments amounted to a *carte blanche* to make money. A person who failed to get rich on such an opportunity within a short period was described as stupid.

In this way, hundreds of young men and women became rich, some of them multi-millionaires, thanks to embezzlement of public funds. There was no accountability and bribery and corruption were rampant. No one, not even the courts, took any cognizance of these evils. Everyone was trying to make money by all possible means. At customs in the airports and harbours, people stopped dealing with officials. Everything was transacted outside the official channels, through middlemen of the officers-in-charge, and from the back door. No efforts were made to hide these goings on. Corruption had become a normal and open activity.

Salaries that government servants received were soon not enough for one week's subsistence. Yet some of them were building house after house or buying farms. From where was the money coming? From embezzlement of public funds, obviously.

At the beginning of the Revolution, life for the people was easier as food was cheap, especially such items as maize and meat. Even spaghetti and rice, which were imported, were affordable on a daily basis for most families.

One innovative step which the Government had taken in the early years was to promote fish consumption. To encourage people to eat fish, the meat markets remained closed on government orders for two days each week (Monday and Thursday). Somalis, most of whom come from a pastoral family tradition, have a strong liking for meat, and eat the meat of the cow, camel, goat and sheep. Only the inhabitants of the coastal areas habitually consumed fish. Other seafood such as lobsters, oysters, prawns, shrimps, crabs and squid were not consumed by Somalis at all, except for a few individuals who had begun eating them whilst in Europe. Not everybody became a lover of fish overnight, but many Somalis who today enjoy fish were probably helped to acquire the taste during this experiment.

After the Ogaden War, the country faced severe food shortages. People with low incomes and the salaried class suffered most. They could not cope with the soaring prices of foodstuffs and other essentials. Decent folk were forced to become corrupt for the sake of their family's survival. A gentleman might stare at you, embarrassed to ask for help, or even an old friend or a colleague who earlier had been able to manage quite well. Cooking in most houses in the capital is done on charcoal, so if neighbours did not notice signs of a fire for several days, it meant the inmates of the house did not have food to cook.

I lived near the orientation centre of Hamar Jab Jab and the leading lights among his 'disciples' at the Centre knew that, as Chief of Protocol I had easy access to the President. So they rarely asked me to attend the compulsory weekly meetings of the residents of the area. However, I was not so lucky as to be excused when they were collecting contributions in the neighbourhood.

My womenfolk attended the weekly meetings for the ladies, and there they obtained a ration card for buying essential commodities, including food items, from the government fair price

The way 'Revolution Day' was celebrated: tight security.

Party Members saying "Yes".

shops. The prices in the open market were very high, but we were able to get basic supplies of rice, oil, sugar and spaghetti from the shop at the Centre. The rations were not enough to live on unless supplemented from the open market, but in theory the rations were an excellent measure for equitably distributing the meagre supplies of food available to the nation. The rationing system worked quite well in the beginning, but like everything else, it too became a means for embezzlement.

Later, it was only a massive refugee presence from neighbouring countries that prevented many Somalis from dying of hunger. Food assistance for the refugees was used to keep the whole country afloat. Apart from deliberate diversion by Government of refugee food aid to a favoured few to sell in the open market, a huge black market trade sprung up around the refugee camps, involving merchants, speculators and refugees alike in re-distribution of US and EEC refugee aid. The entire country had been reduced to a sort of refugee camp.

The Supreme Revolutionary Council had also promised to eradicate disease. In the capital there were three hospitals—one general hospital built with the assistance of the European Community, the second a maternity hospital built by the People's Republic of China, and the third was the old Forlanini Hospital, also known as Lazzaretti, and meant for mentally sick and tuberculosis patients.

During the fifties and sixties, Mogadishu also had a small but rather well maintained hospital called Ospedale Maurizio Rava. Later, I do not know for what reason, the building was transformed into offices of the Ministry of Health. One thing I do know is that our Governments never possessed a maintenance mentality. They used a building until it collapsed for lack of maintenance and care, and then just moved to another one. This is why we could not even retain what had been left behind by the colonial powers.

The Revolutionary regime made no investment in any of these hospitals. On the contrary, it allowed a steep decline and deterioration in their overall maintenance. Broken beds, unclean bedsheets and towels—if bedsheets and towels could be found at all—dirty floors, ceilings and walls, unhygienic toilets all contributed to an altogether sickening atmosphere that would make even a healthy man ill. Though the hospitals had been reduced to garbage dumps, not having any other alternative, the people had to be content with them. Family attendants brought medicines from outside for the sick; they brought food which they had cooked at home; they brought bed linen and bandages; some even brought their own 'nafta' (diesel oil) for the hospital generator, so that the surgeon could use the operating theatre.

Mogadishu also had a small hospital run by the Police Force and built primarily for the use of their people. Non-police force families had to pay for the facilities. The hospital, which was like a private nursing home, also had a wing set aside for Party members, and the expenses incurred by them were borne by the Government. The Party members commonly went to the police hospital to relax at government expense. As for genuine medical treatment or for medical checks, all the privileged people were sent to Europe or America at State expense.

Those going abroad for medical checks, were given hard currency. The President approved the requests for funds, always in large amounts, sufficient for the person, his wife and for one or two children to fly off for an extended vacation in luxurious surroundings—a respite from their dreary poverty-stricken homeland. They would take the money and go to Rome, Paris, Bonn or Washington. There they would go to a private hospital or nursing home for a medical check-up, and as much of the money as possible went into their private bank accounts. If serious medical attention was called for, the bills for this were usually passed on to the local embassy for payment, as were the bills for their expensive five-star hotels or rented luxury apartments. That was how the revolutionary regime was eradicating the menace of disease.

It is quite true what everyone says about Somalis: we are one nation, we speak one language, we worship Allah, we have one culture and we share the same customs. But we are of many tribes.

It is an old practice in Somalia to use tribal affiliation along with a person's name. For many years, it had been common practice when writing letters to people at home or abroad to add the name of the person's tribe after his name when addressing the envelope.

The tribe was part of the address. It was recognition of a person's identity and his lineage. We may have borrowed this custom from the Arab world.

In the past, tribal affiliation played a unifying role in society. It was a source of solidarity among tribesmen, creating a system of mutual assistance for the solution of day-to-day problems among a tribe's members. Each tribe had its respected chiefs and elders, who enjoyed their people's trust and were vested with the authority to resolve disputes. The elders were also the representative of the tribe in any dialogue with other tribal chiefs, and in case of inter-tribal conflicts.

Throughout our history, the Somalis like any other people have had differences among themselves. We have fought each other with sticks and stones, with knives and broken bottles, and with spears. We shot each other with bow and arrow, and finally we have even shot each other with guns. But historically, through the mediation and reconciliation of our tribal wisemen, our people have come to their senses and solved their problems peacefully.

Tribalism really became harmful when people began using tribal connections for personal gain, to the detriment of others' interests. After independence, the politicians used tribalism in election campaigns and created artificial divisions among the people on tribal lines, threatening the unity of the country. It was the commonest ploy of politicians to use tribal loyalties to promote their own interests.

Like a cancer, if tribalism acquires a malignant form, penetrating the minds of people, they become prisoners of an abhorrent system. A people's representatives elected through tribalism become hostage to the tribal thugs who ensured their election. They would be asked to get money for "their" people, and find jobs for their young boys and girls—however illiterate or incompetent—at the expense of others more qualified. That is what one must expect from a government which is composed of persons elected on the basis of tribalism.

The Somali Youth League Party had tried to abolish tribalism during its early days. The Party did not have much success either in eliminating or mitigating its deleterious influence. The system used by the SYL was to introduce the use of an 'ex-' as a prefix to the tribal nomenclature. However, subsequent governments found tribalism convenient for promoting their political interests, or as an instrument in a policy of divide and rule. Rampant tribalism, nepotism, corruption and malpractice, profiteering and embezzlement of public funds constituted the main reason for the military intervention on 21 October, 1969. And, in its First Charter (Article 5) the Military Government declared that it was duty bound to liquidate corruption, anarchy, tribalism and all forms of social immorality in State activity.

Before the Military takeover, it was rumoured, and widely believed, that the Government had distributed weapons to various tribes to defend themselves from the 'enemy'. God knows if this was true, but it was alleged that tribalism was behind the assassination of the second President of the Republic, Abdirashid Ali Shermarke, in October 1969. Shermarke had been elected President, but who knows how many others had been killed during the election process, for either tribal or personal advantage?

Whether this was a tactical move to consolidate its power or whether it was sincerely committed to liquidating the evil of tribalism from our society, to begin with, the Revolutionary Government did launch a war against it.

The Revolutionary regime tried to combat tribalism by launching a propaganda campaign to educate the people against the monster which was weakening the nation from within. The propaganda office of the SRC made an effigy representing tribalism, and exhorted the people to bury it. On the day of its burial, all important politicians, senior government officials, and the public were invited to witness the event. This was how the Revolutionary Government formally buried tribalism. Some felt it was a childish act, to pretend that tribalism could be buried or burnt in this jocular manner.

The only effective way to combat tribalism, of course, was to treat all people equally before the law of the land, and for the leaders to rise above parochial loyalties and create socio-political conditions under which the people could spontaneously feel equal. In the absence of these measures, and lacking an independent and impartial judiciary committed to upholding social justice, the liquidation of tribalism was to remain a chimera.

God, the Almighty in His Holy Book, the Koran says:

In the Name Of Allah, Most Gracious, Most Merciful.

'O mankind. We created
you from a single (pair)
Of a male and a female,
And made you into Nations and Tribes, that
Ye may know each other,
(Not that you may despise
each other). Verily,
The most honoured of you
In the sight of Allah
Is (he who is) the most
Righteous of you.
And Allah has full knowledge
And is well acquainted
(With all things).' *

In the meantime, the effects of the defeat in the war with Ethiopia were beginning to be felt in the country, and a deteriorating security situation was becoming more evident. As the President felt more insecure he attempted to shore up his position by surrounding himself with those whom he thought he could trust and who were closely related to him.

From time to time one would hear bomb explosions in Mogadishu. I remember a particularly tense moment in the early 1980s, when the Italian Minister of Foreign Affairs, Mr. Emilio Colombo arrived in Mogadishu on an official visit, and there was a bomb explosion outside the Egyptian Embassy. As Chief of Protocol, I was riding in the motorcade with the delegation from the airport to Villa Somalia, where our guest was to be accommodated. Immediately after we left the airport I heard over the police radio-telephone in the car in which I was travelling, that there had just been a bomb explosion near the Egyptian Embassy.

The Egyptian Embassy was situated on the main road at Kilometer 4, which the delegation of the Italian Foreign Minister

*   Sura XLIX [Hujurat] 13

was to pass on its way to the guest house. The Italians knew there was trouble in the country, but it would have been considered a personal attack on them had the explosion taken place when their Foreign Minister was passing the spot. The Security outriders were instructed to avoid Km.4 and take us on another route via the Air Force Headquarters road—Aviazione. For the moment, the visiting dignitary was oblivious of the bomb incident, but by next morning he would positively have heard about it.

The Security Service believed that bombs were being supplied to the opposition groups by some foreign missions in the capital. Though we were not sure, we believed that the countries who had supported Ethiopia in the Ogaden War could be supporting the opposition groups in the country, with a view to destabilizing the regime. The Government consequently decided to control the movements of the diplomatic staff of those countries suspected of having clandestine relations with the opposition. The Security Service was instructed to tighten surveillance over their activities and over those visitors who frequented these foreign missions. Normally, the diplomatic missions and their diplomatic staff enjoyed all the privileges and immunities prescribed by the Vienna Convention on Diplomatic Relations.

All ambassadors or heads of mission had the privilege to enter the VIP salon whenever they came to receive or see off a person or delegation at the airport. This privilege was also enjoyed by Somali dignitaries. Although it was called the VIP Salon, ordinary people also frequented the patio outside the salon, from where they could see their friends going to or coming from the aircraft. Occasionally, people would go out on to the tarmac where the aircraft was parked. It was just like a small local upcountry aerodrome, with no arrival lounge, and with a primitive system for baggage handling.

The airport staff discovered that, under cover of the privilege enjoyed by senior diplomats, a driver of the Soviet Embassy was travelling to the airport in the Ambassador's car, Soviet flag flying, and was entering the gate and driving straight to the aircraft's cargo compartment. There he collected parcels which actually required customs clearance from the Protocol Department of the Ministry of Foreign Affairs. This clandestine operation must have been going on for quite some time before it was discovered, quite by chance.

In view of the deteriorating law and order situation in the capital, and some suspicious activities by staff of diplomatic missions at the airport, the Government's nervousness led them to introduce an inspection system of diplomatic cargo at the entry point. This was done in accordance with Article 36 of the Vienna Convention on Diplomatic Relations, and was to verify all unaccompanied luggage or cargo, or even what the embassies called 'diplomatic goods', by opening them in the presence of the diplomatic agent or his authorized representative'.

A note was sent through the Protocol Department to all diplomatic missions in Mogadishu, informing them of the decision. Although the note went to all missions, the customs and security officers knew very well the missions which were actually being targeted.

One day, the Embassy of the U.S.S.R., whose national airline Aeroflot had regular flights to Mogadishu, called me in the office and asked me to help them get permission from civil aviation to allow two diplomats to travel to Dar-es-Salaam. They had no rights to take on passengers from Mogadishu to Dar-es-Salaam, Tanzania. Only with the authorization of civil aviation could this be done, because other airlines had concessions on this route. I obtained the necessary permission for the diplomats.

From Moscow, the plane made a stopover in Mogadishu, to disembark passengers and unload cargo, before proceeding to Dar-es-Salaam.

The two diplomats who had travelled by their national airline to Dar-es-Salaam returned to Mogadishu by another airline a few days later, bringing with them a huge cargo. We knew that the cargo had originally come from their own country, and had been on the Aeroflot flight that had touched down at Mogadishu a few days earlier, but had not then been offloaded. With the recent tightening up of airport security at Mogadishu, they had apparently thought that cargo coming from a third country and on another airline would avert suspicion. The cargo contained heavy cases which were being closely guarded by embassy officials. The customs people told the embassy men who had come to collect the cargo that they would like to verify the contents to see whether they corresponded to the list that the embassy had presented to the customs officers.

The Diplomats informed their ambassador of what was happening at the airport, and the case reached the authorities in the Foreign Ministry. In the meantime, the Soviet ambassador sent more personnel to the airport to guard the cargo. Airport security on its part also deployed more people to make sure that the diplomats did not use force to take away the cargo.

The Protocol Department made it clear to the embassy that there were serious grounds for presuming that the cargo contained articles not covered by the privileges granted to them, and that, therefore, the cargo was subject to inspection, in the presence of the USSR Ambassador, or his authorized representative.

The embassy refused to accept inspection by the customs officers and the day passed without break in the stalemate. Next day, the two sides changed guards, but not positions. Our side told the ambassador that if the cargo could not be verified, the embassy could transport it back to the country of its origin. Four or five days later, the embassy decided to re-export the cargo to its original country, and it left our customs premises for the airline.

Many countries were suspected to be secretly supporting the clandestine opposition, and those with embassies in Mogadishu were therefore kept under surveillance by Security, and anyone found entering the embassy of a country considered hostile was severely punished.

At the end of the Ogaden War, the Siad regime found that it had virtually no friends. The countries of the Eastern Bloc and Cuba had adopted an extremely hostile attitude towards us during the war itself. In a way it had been a war which the Soviets had enticed us into, perhaps as a means for punishing Somalia for its refusal to submit to their mediatory role, and for eventually throwing them out of the country. As far as the West was concerned, it maintained a neutral or passive stance towards the Ogaden War, even though its interests had been severely hurt in Ethiopia. Our attempts to mend fences with the United States bore no fruits, exemplified by the US Administration's refusal to allow Iran to extend military assistance to Somalia. This is not to deny that humanitarian assistance for refugees continued to pour in from the West.

Insignia of the Somali Revolutionary
Socialist Party.

CHAPTER XII

In Khartoum

I enjoyed working at Protocol, travelling to different countries with the President and other dignitaries. At times, it was a tiresome and a demanding job, but it had its rewards too. It provided me numerous opportunities to meet international leaders, diplomats and experts, besides, of course, enabling me to know our own leaders more intimately. Protocol was considered a thankless job, but I found it enlightening.

After 22 years in Government service, including 15 years with the Ministry of Foreign Affairs, I was appointed Ambassador to the Sudan in 1982. Having begun working at the rank of an Attache in 1968, I now found myself at the summit of my professional career. I once again offered my humble gratitude to Allah, the Almighty.

At this point of time, the Sudan was considered an important posting from the viewpoint of our national interests in the region. The Somali Mission in the Sudan was expected to oversee the developments in Ethiopia with which we had had no diplomatic relations since the outbreak of the Ogaden War on 23 July 1977. Khartoum was therefore considered the ideal place for Ethiopia-watching.

As there was a broad convergence in our (negative) perspective on the Ethiopian regime of Mengistu, both the Sudan and Somalia were believed to be supporting Ethiopian dissidents. We were reported to be providing moral and material assistance to the Eriterean, Tigrean, Oromo and other liberation fronts. It was well known to the world that Ethiopia, with the tacit approval of its patrons, the USSR and Cuba, had been extending full support including bases on its soil to various groups fighting against the central governments in Mogadishu and in Khartoum.

One of the most galling irritants for the regime in Somalia was the anti-government propaganda from the so-called 'mobile radio', named Radio Halgan, and controlled and operated by the

Somali rebel opposition. The regime in Somalia believed that these 'anti-revolutionaries' were broadcasting from the old Radio Voice of the Gospel in Addis Ababa. Whatever radio station they were using, they certainly touched a raw nerve of the Siad regime in Mogadishu. The rebels were using the enemy of their enemy as an ally, in the hatred campaign against the Mogadishu regime.

The Ethiopian Embassy in Khartoum had a strong security section whose duty it was to monitor the activities of the Eritrean liberation movements, the Tigre liberation movement, the Oromo liberation front and other Ethiopian opposition groups with offices in the Sudan. The Ethiopian security network had many people, including hotel waiters, on its pay roll.

Other common factors bringing Sudan and Somalia together were that both countries had military regimes which had come to power by toppling civilian administrations, and at approximately the same time, and both had an orientation towards the Eastern Bloc countries led by Russia. Both President Mohamed Siad Barre and President Jafar Mohamed Nimeri had established personal dictatorships with the support of a one-party system instituted by them during their first few years in power. Their early performance has been judged to be relatively good, providing stability and a respite from the internecine struggles of various parochial groups that was characteristic of the civilian regimes. However, as time passed, the two leaders became obsessed with the idea that they alone were the saviours of their people, though in fact they had lost touch with reality and had become addicts to flattery and sycophancy.

The Sudan, the largest country in Africa, has abundant water resources from the Blue and White Niles. In the Arab world, the Sudan is called 'the bread basket of the Arabs'. In fact, the Arabs have poured in enormous investments for agricultural and poultry development. The Sudan has abundant livestock, which is exported to neighbouring countries. Notwithstanding all these assets, the common man often found it difficult to procure food at affordable prices.

The Sudan had a well established system of education. Its institutions of higher studies turn out highly qualified people every year, but due to lack of economic incentives and poor employment opportunities at home, there was much 'brain drain', with most educated Sudanese going to the countries in the Gulf for employment, though some of them also left the country for political reasons.

The Diplomatic Corps was large in Khartoum. Almost all the countries of the East and West, of the Arab World, and of Africa and Asia were represented there.

Occasionally, while in Khartoum, I wrote articles on problems in the Horn of Africa and on the Ethiopian policies of oppression against the people it had colonized. Sometimes, the newspapers would not entertain my articles for publication. Sometimes I was lucky and had the opportunity to make my views known through the Sudanese press.

Some of the Ambassadors of countries of the Eastern Bloc such as Czechoslovakia, the then-German Democratic Republic, and Bulgaria called upon me individually to discuss developments in the Horn. Obviously, they wanted to know whether there had been any change in Somalia's policy since the Ogaden War, in which they had been on the Ethiopian side. Whether they had been sent by their elder brother Russia or had come on their own, was difficult to determine, but they must have been reporting our discussions to the Russians.

The Czechoslovak diplomat was well acquainted with the situation as he had spent some time in Ethiopia before coming to the Sudan. He once told me that he had visited the Ogaden region when he was in Ethiopia only to discover that the Region's population was all Somali and they had nothing in common with the Ethiopians.

To each of the diplomats that I met in my office, I gave a collection of documents relating to the situation in the Ogaden, for their perusal. The Bulgarian Ambassador came to see me twice, and on the second occasion he had in his hand a book that I had given him when he had visited me first. He opened it to a page and asked, "Why does your country not accept the Resolution of the Organization of African Unity adopted at the Summit Conference in Cairo in 1964 which calls upon Member States to respect existing boundaries?"

I explained my country's immovable position, to the effect that we rejected the Resolution because it recognized colonial boundaries. We Somalis rejected the colonialists themselves, how then could we accept boundaries that the colonialists demarcated for us? The Resolution was conveniently acceptable to countries which had been given territories of others by the colonialists, but the Cairo Resolution infringed our territorial rights. We were among its victims.

I did not know whether the Bulgarian Envoy was satisfied with my answer or not, but he did not ask me any further question. In any case, the Somali position had not changed as a result of the Ogaden War. Though we had been defeated in the Ogaden War it was by forces that the Soviet Union had brought from the 'Socialist Camp', not by Mengistu's forces. The Cubans had brought their troops from Angola to Ethiopia to fight against the Somalis. A Cuban Diplomat once told me in Dar-es-Salaam, that "for the Cubans that was a very hard war".

A few days later their Chief, the Soviet Ambassador expressed a desire to call upon me. We were now in 1983. Can you imagine a Soviet Ambassador calling on a Somali Ambassador? I told my secretary to inform his secretary that His Excellency was most welcome to come at any time he wished. We agreed upon a mutually convenient date to meet in my embassy. Surprisingly, he came without an escort. Soviet ambassadors normally went everywhere with an escort, who was usually presented as an interpreter—like old men unable to manage without a walking stick. But on this occasion he came alone.

I received him in my little 6 x 4 metre office. I asked His Excellency to sit on the sofa. The usual biscuits, peanuts and candy were ready to be served on the coffee table. On the surface, all was very sweet, but on my mind were the very bitter recollections of remarks made by one of his Russian colleagues who, subsequent to my Government's decision to expel the Russians from our country, had threatened: "we will bring you to your knees".

When he entered and we had sat down for coffee, his questioning was direct. "What do you want from Ethiopia?" he asked me, just like that, without any introductory remarks and in a very undiplomatic manner. He could behave like this because he was an ambassador of a great power.

"We want nothing from Ethiopia," I said, "We only want that Ethiopia should vacate the region it colonizes." I continued, "We are Socialists, Ethiopia is Socialist. Our common mentor, Comrade Lenin taught that a socialist country should not colonize another socialist country. And I think, Excellency, that you also agree with Comrade Lenin." He did not answer.

I continued speaking, undiplomatically, adopting the tone with which he had begun our meeting. "You Russians must have seen in your military records what the Somalis were capable of. If the military experts and troops of the Soviet Union and its allies, including the Cubans, had not engaged in the War, you know what we could have done to the Ethiopians. In war, someone has to lose. Today you are with them [Ethiopia] and so it is to you that I say, tell them to let the people of the Ogaden go free. Before you, there were others, who have now left, as you too are bound to leave the area. And the moment you leave the people will rise again." I ended with a proverbial kind of statement:

"You are like the broom and the Somalis are the ground. The broom will perish and the ground will remain."

"You are an arrogant man," he said to me.

"No sir, I am only proud," I told him.

That was our conversation. Rough and unfriendly. When he had sought an appointment with me I had thought that, although we were still at war we could have a civil dialogue with each other. I did not expect that we should be talking about a future reconciliation between our two countries; I knew it was too soon for that. But I had thought that four Ambassadors from Socialist countries, including the Soviet Union, calling on me should have some significance. I had anticipated a probable attempt to pave the way for improving the atmosphere between us. I had not expected that he was visiting me to make me more angry. He did not even give a parting smile, as we usually do when we call upon fellow ambassadors.

The Sudan was considered a very difficult posting by diplomats. But for me, as I hailed from a place where the situation was worse than in Khartoum, it was not very inconvenient. Khartoum was hotter than Mogadishu and the extraordinary *hubbub* dust storms which periodically hit the city penetrated the windows and doors, to enter wardrobes and cupboards, covering everything with a film of yellow.

The *hubbub* storms lasted from mid-June to mid-July, during which time the embassies avoided holding garden parties. The Sudanese people welcomed the cool weather which the dust-storms brought for short periods. The dust appeared like a huge mountain moving across the sky. Sometimes it caused delay or diversion of aircraft bound for Khartoum. Although Mogadishu did not have these Sahara dust storms, it had many other things in common with Khartoum. Power shortages was one. In fact, I felt very much at home whenever I walked along Republic Street, *Shari al Jamhuriya,* and saw power generators on the doorsteps of the shops. Other familiar conditions were the shortages of certain food items, and sometimes of petrol.

What was a totally uncommon sight to me, however, were the public protests. I was surprised to observe demonstrations, organized and held by the Sudanese people, against price increases on items such as bread or petrol. I was amazed to see that they would confront the police with stones. That kind of thing never happened in Somalia. There the Government would increase prices by any amount and no one dared to speak openly against it. Merchants could sell their goods at any price, would reduce the size of a loaf of bread and at the same time increase its price, and no one would open his mouth. Harsh punishment awaited those who tried to protest or demonstrate against speculators. The Government would not tolerate demonstrations for fear they would escalate into anti-government protests.

Both the Sudan and Somalia were ruled by generals who had captured power through military coups. Both believed that their countries needed nationalist dictators like themselves. They believed army officers were more disciplined, more organized and more patriotic than the civilians. They believed that the Army, which defends the country from enemies both external and internal, also had the right to rule the country.

From the mid-1960s and through the 1970s Africa saw a rash of self-appointed military regimes come to power. In most cases where the soldiers had captured power from civilian governments, they were hailed by the people, excluding the prosperous elite section of society which had had close links with the earlier corrupt governments. The military men presented themselves as defenders of the interests of the exploited masses and, to begin with, the people too perceived them in that guise.

Generally, the armed forces did a fair job for the first three to five years, during which period they were kept busy demonstrating that they were sincerely serving the country and the people, and effecting tangible corrections. But after that, they commonly began working for themselves, their relatives and their tribes.

A civilian who is not honest knows that he has a maximum period of four or five years before the next election, and within this period he must do what he can for himself. As for an honest politician, you might find him at the end of his term in the same house, not having made any fortune whatsoever. An army officer who captures power by the barrel of the gun believes that he has risked his life for that power, therefore he has the right to keep it as long as he can. He is afraid of his colleagues, does not trust anyone, including sometimes his own family. He imagines that people like himself might come with a gun and take his power away from him. So, he forgets the promises he made to the people and the country when he came to power. His own survival becomes more important than anything else and, to ensure that, he builds defensive fences around himself, by appointing members of his family and his tribe to key positions and amassing wealth in foreign banks for future safety. The man who once said that he was from the people and for the people builds barricades to keep his own people away from him. The more fear grows in him, the more violent he becomes. His power becomes a disease which eventually kills him or forces him to flee the country or abandon power, in disgrace. Army officers who usurp power by staging a coup d'etat—or by revolution as they usually wish to call it—most often lie to the people. They promise to hold elections shortly when taking over power, but such promises are never fulfilled.

Unlike Somalia, which has a homogeneous population, united by the egalitarian message of Islam, the Sudan's inhabitants in the North differ in experience, culture and religion from those in the South, Islam being the religion of a large majority of people in the North, while in the South some are Christians, and others are animists.

Prior to 1983, the Sudan was a secular state, but in September 1983, the then-President Jafar Mohamed Nimeri introduced the Sharia Law (Islamic Law) which added fuel to an already inflamed situation in Southern Sudan. The application of Sharia Law for the entire population of the country, irrespective of religious belief, alienated and infuriated the population of the South. The provisions for stringent punishment for theft, adultery and consumption of alcohol under Islamic Law were resented by the non-Islamic segments of the population.

During the promulgation ceremony which took place in front of the Grand Hotel of Khartoum, Nimeri publicly destroyed and poured a large quantity of alcoholic beverages, valued at millions of US dollars, into the Nile.

"Even the fish got drunk and jumped out of the river", was the joke of the day.

People wondered how Nimeri who was not so devout himself had suddenly become what some termed a Muslim fanatic. He established special courts for the quick processing of cases and handing down of sentences. He constituted a force which was given full power to arrest anyone it considered a sinner. Stories abounded of their zealous actions—jumping over house fences and arresting innocent people who were enjoying a peaceful evening at home with their families. It was rumoured that this special security force was implicating people who never touched wine, by placing bottles of alcohol in their gardens. It was said that an Italian priest had been arrested from within his Church on the grounds that he was not only drinking wine but was also serving it to the people who had assembled there for communion service. It was also reported that some foreigners were arrested and lashed, accused of adultery with the women companions in their homes. Some of the stories were of doubtful authenticity, but they did capture the mood in the capital at the time.

It was certainly true that there were instances of diplomats' residences being searched 'by mistake', which caused us to band together and put a sign on our doors in both Arabic and English indicating that it was a diplomat's house, to prevent uncalled-for intrusions.

Introduction of the Sharia Law, or the September Law as it came to be known, was received variously. Some welcomed it because of their firm religious conviction of its rightness; some hitherto opposition groups in the country welcomed it as a right step; and there were others who welcomed it because they thought that by introducing Sharia Law, Nimeri had dug his own grave. In Western Europe, it was interpreted as a hostile measure against the Sudanese Christians who were getting support from the Christian churches around the world. For many Sudanese, though, it was a restriction they would prefer to do without. Consumption of alcoholic drinks—whiskey and beer—was commonplace. People would drink discreetly in their homes or at a friend's house without making nuisances of themselves. Nevertheless, their fondness for a drop of alcohol was underlined in popular jokes such as:

During the course of a party, when the call to prayer is heard, a Sudanese will just say 'Please put some more ice in my glass, I will return in a moment after offering prayers'; or, The Sudanese break their fast during the month of Ramadan with a pint of beer.

When Nimeri banned the sale and consumption of alcohol, illicit brewing houses predictably flourished and the sale of black market alcohol was thriving in different parts of Khartoum. Ethiopian immigrants who brewed their own national alcoholic drink *tatch* for their own compatriots, found new consumers and a new market for their product.

Those who did not consume alcohol were not at all bothered by the September Law, and those who were its addicts somehow managed to procure alcohol in spite of the ban.

There are many Muslim countries in the world and none of them makes as much public clamour about exercising the Sharia Law. Nimeri invited uncalled-for criticism from within and outside the country. The September Law served to deepen the political crisis for a government which was already facing a serious threat from rebellious elements in the southern part of the country.

Both General Mohamed Siad Barre and General Jafar Mohamed Nimeri had usurped power in 1969. General Nimeri had captured power on, 25 May, and his takeover was popularly referred to as 'The May Revolution'. After his fall, it was dubbed by his own former Foreign Minister, Dr. Mansur Khaled, as "The Revolution of DisMay"—it was the title of the book he wrote following the fall of Nimeri.

The Sudan is a very rich country. Besides its agricultural

potential, there was also the black gold—oil—discovered around Bantyu, South Sudan. I was there when the 14 so-called 'unity wells' were drilled and thick black liquid was ready to be shipped through Port Sudan to the world market. The production had to be stopped because of the civil war in the country. The Chevron Oil Company which was working in that area had to leave the country for security reasons. They left for Somalia thinking that the Company would be more secure there. Here too, they had to leave due to civil war.

Both these countries' peoples would have enjoyed a better and more prosperous life if only stability and peace had prevailed.

In Somalia, Mohamed Siad Barre had captured power on 21 October 1969, that is in the same month in which Lenin had masterminded the Great Bolshevik Revolution in 1917 in Russia. In the first Constitution of Somalia, there was an article which said, 'Islam is the religion of the State'. Unlike the Sudan or certain other countries of Africa, virtually the entire population of Somalia is of one religion. In its First Charter, which had seven articles on internal policy and six on foreign policy, the Revolution had completely ignored religion. In the Second Charter too, no mention was made of religion. Instead, it had an article which said, 'The Somali Democratic Republic will adopt scientific socialism...'

It was quite apparent that the Revolution was attempting to distance itself from religion. On 11 January 1975, the Government issued what it called The Family Law, *Xeerka Qoyska*, encompassing within it some provisions which were not compatible with the Koran. This caused an outburst of anger among the masses and particularly among the religious leaders. The latter delivered speeches in the mosques protesting against the Law.

The President refused to repeal the Family Law, and considering the protests a challenge to his authority, ordered the arrest of those he considered trouble-makers. The accused were tried in a special court, which was a mockery of justice, and eleven persons—religious leaders and sheikhs—were sentenced to death. It was an incredible verdict, and the population was stunned. These people had committed no crime, they had not taken up arms to fight against the government or caused injury or death to anyone. They had expressed an opinion on a matter which was everybody's concern. Appeals for clemency to spare their lives came from many quarters including a number of Islamic countries. The President, the 'Father of the Nation' who had the power to arrest and to release, to sentence and to pardon, ignored all the calls for clemency and confirmed the court verdict.

The 15 January 1975 was a sad and sorrowful day for all Somalis. The eleven men, who had only voiced their opinion in defence of their faith, were lined up at the stake—*tiirka,* their hands tied behind their backs, their legs tied, and their eyes blindfolded with black cloth, and they were executed by a firing squad, which fired at them until each of them was dead. The whole country was shocked. The Islamic world condemned the mass execution as a barbaric and inhuman act.

In Sudan, the policies adopted by Nimeri might have been easier to apply in a totally Muslim country, but for a country like the Sudan where about one third of the people are non-Muslim, the adoption of the Sharia Law invited strong resentment and protests. Both Nimeri and Siad in diametrically opposite ways had acted inadvisedly, at the cost of their nations.

The security network of the Ethiopian Embassy in Khartoum was led by the Counsellor of the Embassy. He was of Somali origin. We knew each other, but whenever we met at cocktails he avoided talking with me in Somali. I was never sure whether this was because of his loyalty to the Ethiopian regime or whether he was afraid someone might report it to his ambassador and that he would be considered anti-Ethiopian by his masters. The Sudan and Ethiopia did not have good relations, and harboured each others' rebel groups. Yet this Counsellor seemed to move freely everywhere in the country. I once asked the Sudanese Security, with whom we had very good relations and a 'common enemy' in Ethiopia, why they did not restrict the activities of the man, and was told that his financial resources were such that he could overcome most obstacles that were put in his way.

This 'Somali' Counsellor at the Ethiopian Embassy in Khartoum had two brothers, one of whom lived in Djibouti and the other in Somalia. The one who was from Djibouti was at that time Djibouti's ambassador to Saudi Arabia and the other was a director general in the Foreign Ministry of Somalia, and later to become Somalia's ambassador to Lagos. Three Somali brothers were citizens of three different countries, working in sensitive posts for three different governments. The Ethiopian Government was soon to nominate this man of Somali origin as Ambassador to Saudi Arabia, where his other brother was already serving as Ambassador of Djibouti. For whatever reason, the Saudis as it happened rejected his nomination. Later he was sent instead as Ethiopia's Ambassador to Libya.

Somalia and the Sudan had some common enemies and common friends. As Libya was reported to be supporting certain opposition groups in the Sudan, relations between the two countries were very tense. There were reports in Khartoum that as many as 30,000 Sudanese dissidents were receiving training and instruction in Tripoli. We too did not have good relations with Libya as a result of the support it gave to Ethiopia during the war in the Ogaden. Both countries, Somalia and Sudan, had good relations with Egypt, which was also not on good terms with Libya. The Sudan and Somalia, as well as Oman were the only three countries that did not break off diplomatic relations with Egypt in 1979 when Anwar Sadat signed the Camp David Agreement with Israel. Sudan had closer historical ties with Egypt, and during this period President Nimeri was working particularly hard to realize the goal of *Al Takamul,* or integration, between the two countries. He fervently wanted to unite the two peoples of the Nile. A popular song dedicated to integration ended with the words: "The Sudan is for Egypt and Egypt is for the Sudan".

The people of the Sudan, however, were very skeptical about the goal of integrating the two countries. The opponents of the idea were of the opinion that if it succeeded, Egyptian farmers, who were known to be hard workers, would swarm the country and take over the farming activities.

Of course, the Sudanese would not go to Cairo to farm but thousands of Sudanese students would go there for higher education. If the integration move succeeded, the flow of students was bound to increase. Egypt already had a well established branch of Cairo University in Khartoum, which was run by the Egyptians. It admitted 3000 students annually, while Khartoum University admitted only 1000 a year.

Nimeri was like the monsoon which sometimes blows from one direction and sometime from the opposite. He generally supported the Eritrean cause, but sometimes took action detrimental to their interests. Once, his coastal guards in the Red Sea stopped a boat carrying Somali assistance to the Eritreans. When I could not persuade the Sudanese authorities to release the boat, a special envoy had to come from Somalia to meet President Nimeri, bearing a personal message from the Somali President requesting Nimeri to release the boat for its onward destination.

One morning in 1984, one of my friends came to my office, as he did from time to time. He stood across my desk and asked me: "Do you know who the Fallashas are?"

"Yes. They are the black Jews who live in Ethiopia," I answered.

He proceeded to tell me a story he had heard about a plan to secretly transfer the Fallashas from Ethiopia to Israel via Khartoum airport. Ethiopia, Israel, Sudan and the USA, and also some other countries, were said to be involved in the matter.

My house was located not far from the Airport. It was actually on a street parallel to the runway, and it had a terrace from where I could observe aircraft landing and taking off. Undoubtedly, as the world was to find out later, the operation did take place, and from my home I nightly heard the noise of aircraft in much greater volume than was usual. The planes carrying the Fallashas were flown after midnight, in a top secret operation, code named Operation Moses. At this time Khartoum lived with an overnight curfew which came into operation at 10 o'clock every night—a factor which could help disguise unusual movements and activity around the airport. The operation was said to have been going on from February to November 1984. The final flights were made on US C-130s directly from Gadaref in the Eastern Region, and not from Khartoum.

Later it was revealed that Sudan's then-Vice President, who was also Head of the National Security Service, General Omar Mohamed El Tayeb, had authorized the use of Khartoum Airport and Sudanese territory for the transfer of the Fallashas, in agreement with the United States Embassy in Khartoum. Since the Sudan had no relations with Israel, the Americans, on Israel's behalf, had negotiated all the arrangements with the Sudanese officials. Of course, Nimeri must have given the 'go ahead' to his Vice-President.

General El Tayeb visited the United States of America, probably as a reward for his services in the Operation. On 4 March 1985 George Bush who was then Vice President of the United States of America came to the Sudan on an official visit and toured the Eastern Regions where he visited the refugee camps as well. Three weeks later, President Jafar Mohamed Nimeri left for the United States. It was to be his last departure, and a one-way trip. He never returned home either as President or as a private citizen—but more about this later in the chapter.

Once, Khartoum was badly hit by a shortage of petrol and its whole transport system ground to a halt. As a result, the students who largely depended on public transport to go to school and college were put to great inconvenience. The students took to the streets in organized protest and threw stones at cars that were still plying the streets. The demonstrations went on for days. On one morning, foreign diplomats had been attending a government function, and as they left a large crowd of disgruntled students shouting and marching on the streets began pelting stones at the cars, and many ambassadors had their windscreens smashed. I was a little fortunate in that my car escaped the fury of the students.

Among the student demonstrators there were a number of anti-Nimeri groups which had seized on the opportunity to fan the flames of protest against his regime. Although Nimeri's policies and behaviour had become more and more extreme, and his friendship could not be relied upon, his continuation in power at that time was useful for us, as he was the enemy of our enemies and the friend of our friends. However hard it may be to swallow, the well-known maxim about a country having no permanent friends but only permanent interests, is sadly true, and in politics and for the sake of national interests, one is often in a position of having to support 'a necessary evil'. This was my view vis-à-vis Nimeri.

I felt that, in order to enable him to overcome the shortage of oil the Saudis and the Kuwaitis should be prevailed upon to help him out of the crisis. My contention was that, if Nimeri was overthrown his successors might change Sudan's policy towards its neighbouring countries—Ethiopia, Egypt and Libya—and that might not be in Somalia's interests. Those who were opposing Nimeri had trained in countries which were inimical to us. Nimeri had been supporting the right to self-determination of the Somalis under Ethiopian occupation. He was at odds with those countries who were hostile to Somalia. My own Foreign Ministry was not of my view. I was asked not to worry about any developments in the Sudan. Even if there was an attempted coup, I was not to bother. This was the advice I received from Mogadishu.

At the end of March 1985, I was asked by the Ministry of Foreign Affairs of Somalia to attend an Organization of African Unity meeting of the African Ministers of Information in Addis Ababa, Ethiopia. At the time, we had no diplomatic relations with Ethiopia. They could not, of course, prevent a Somali official going to Addis Ababa for an OAU Conference, but what they did was to to make it difficult, for example they would refuse Somali officials permission to fly on their aircraft. From Khartoum, Ethiopian Airlines had a direct flight to Addis Ababa. The alternative way to reach Addis Ababa was to take a Kenyan or a Sudanese flight and change planes in Nairobi.

I asked the Ethiopian Airlines Office to book a seat for me on their carrier, but as expected, they refused to do so. I then called the Ethiopian Embassy, for the first time during the two years of my stay in Khartoum, asking them to instruct the Airline to carry me since I was going to the OAU meeting. Apparently, the embassy told the airlines office to get clearance from their headquarters, for within two days I was informed that I could fly to Addis Ababa by Ethiopian Airlines.

We had no embassy in Addis Ababa, and the two countries—Somalia and Ethiopia—were still in a state of war. During the flight, none of the hostesses or stewards spoke to me. There were security guards on the plane; I was familiar with that from my own country's adoption of Soviet-style strategies. The cabin staff did not offer me any of the hospitality due to me as a passenger. It is possible that, had they shown me due courtesy they would have got into trouble. By the end of the flight I was beginning to feel I had undertaken a suicide mission.

Upon my arrival at Addis airport, I was received by an officer of the protocol section of the OAU. To my great surprise, I found that the Ethiopian Ambassador to the Sudan, Mr. Yilma Tedessa, had also come to welcome me, but with the title of Director of the African Department in the Ministry of Foreign Affairs of Ethiopia. He was still his country's ambassador to the Sudan, but it appeared that this new and interim title provided him a perfect opportunity to meet with the range of African leaders who visited OAU headquarters, and by so doing to lobby for his candidacy for OAU Assistant Secretary General—a post which he did later succeed to.

They had booked me a room in the Hilton Hotel. The Security people were aware of my programme, as I had informed the OAU Secretariat that I would be coming to attend the meeting. At the reception, while I was filling in the check-in form, I paused and looked casually around the lobby. I noticed some men staring at me. The receptionist gave me a key for a room on the fourth floor. I had been forewarned by friends that security people entered the rooms during an occupant's absence to search suitcases and so on. I took my key and went up by the lift to the fourth floor.

The OAU meeting was scheduled to begin the day after my arrival. In the morning, before leaving the room, I decided not to lock my suitcase, the Samsonite which my friends had warned me was likely to be searched during my absence. To make their task easier and to save my suitcase from being forced open, I not only left it unlocked but wide open. Of course, I had taken out all my documents and valuables. I then proceeded to the meeting at OAU Headquarters. When I returned there was no observable evidence that my things had been tampered with.

The next day I had a visitor. As the meeting was to commence an hour later than originally scheduled, I had stayed on in my room. I locked my door from inside with the chain while I went over some documents in preparation for the meeting. I heard a fumbling at the door, somebody was trying to open it from the outside. I rushed over to release the chain and open the door. A man with a towel on his arm, looking like a waiter, was standing there.

"Sorry Sir, I have come to clean the room," he said.

I looked at him and at his little towel. He did not have the normal trolley-table on which room cleaners bring the clean linen and cleaning equipment.

"Have you come to clean my room with one small towel?" I asked him. He was clearly embarrassed and hurried away without giving me a reply. Obviously, he had not been informed about the change in the schedule.

On returning from the meeting that day after dinner, I went to the Bar for a soft drink and to watch a folk dance performance. Two girls pulled their chairs towards my table. "Are you a Somali?" one of them asked me.

"Yes," I said.

"We want to go to Somalia as refugees,"the other girl said.

I looked at them and said, "The Somali borders are open for you, and you know where they are." If they had not been from the secret service they would not have dared to sit at my table in public in the first place.

Moments later, I retired to my room and went to bed hoping to sleep well. I recited a few verses of the Koran before getting under the blanket. No sooner had I closed my eyes than the telephone rang. I picked up the receiver, but nobody spoke. I replaced the receiver. A few hours later, while I was sleeping, the sound of the telephone bell disturbed me again. I picked up the receiver to sense only the vacuum of an empty line. Exasperated, I called reception to complain, I could not tell them not to put calls through, because of the possibility of important calls from Mogadishu, or from my embassy in Khartoum.

The next morning before I left, the woman who came to clean the room said she wanted to ask me something.

"Yes, what is it?"

"I need 20 American dollars to buy something from the duty-free shop and I can give you Ethiopian birr in exchange," she said.

"No problem," I told her, but said I would give them to her later when I came back from the meeting. At that particular moment I could not be bothered to deal with her request. I was annoyed with what they had been doing, dogging my every footstep. Although I had come prepared for a cold welcome in Addis Ababa, it was testing my endurance at every moment. At the venue of the Meeting, there was no cause to complain. The Ethiopian staff at the Organization behaved very well, but at the Hotel the staff did everything to make my stay miserable.

Later that afternoon, the lady cleaner was waiting for me in the corridor outside my room. There were two other girls standing apart at a little distance.

I opened the door to my room. "Come in," I told her. I took US $20 from my pocket and handed it over.

In her hand she had some money, which she wanted to give me. "This is the equivalent in our money. You have done me a big favour."

"Keep it, I do not need it," I said. "Don't worry, I am not an exchange office. Take it as a gift," I added. She was delighted, and could not hide her pleasure.

To avoid any misunderstanding, I had kept the door wide open. Expressing her gratitude, she walked away towards her friends who were waiting in the corridor.

The treatment I received in Addis reflected the attitude of our two countries towards each other. Even during the period in the sixties when official diplomatic relations existed between our countries those relations were never smooth. The Diplomatic Missions in each others' capital were kept under surveillance. Diplomats on both sides were followed closely by secret service officers. Nationals of one country who visited the embassy of the other, were sometimes interrogated and even arrested. It was not very difficult to understand why the tension persisted, we had been in conflict with each other for centuries. I could hardly recall a moment in our modern history when we had normal relations. And so long as the Ethiopians insisted on keeping the Ogaden under their control, the possibility of establishing good neighbourly relations between our two countries was remote.

I left Addis Ababa on 5 April 1985 for Khartoum, via Nairobi, by a flight of the Kenyan Airways, and arrived in Khartoum on the same evening.

Next morning at 10 o'clock, the Sudanese Radio in a special news bulletin announced that the President Jafar Mohamed

Nimeri had been toppled in a bloodless military *coup d'état*. Led by the Chief of Staff, General Abdurahman Swaradaheb, the coup had been staged at a time when President Nimeri was in Cairo on his way back from a visit to the United States. He was asked by the new leadership not to return home. General Swaradaheb had constituted a 15-Member Provisional Military Council and assumed the office of President.

The new President was a very soft spoken person. I had visited him in his office when he was Chief of Staff. At the end of our conversation, I had jokingly remarked that there was a particular moment in time in the life of the Sudanese when Sudan was vulnerable, and its enemies could conveniently attack it then. Taken by surprise, he had asked me what I meant.

"At 10 o'clock in the morning, when everybody in the country has his breakfast and all other activities come to a stop," I had said to him.

In the Sudan, at least in Khartoum, I noticed that even surgeons in hospitals did not perform operations when breakfast time approached. The usual breakfast consisted of big red beans, *ful* in Arabic, with bread and vegetables—fresh tomatoes and lettuce. They ate mostly in groups and from a single bowl. The *ful* is boiled with water and flavoured with onion and garlic and left on the fire for a long time, until it becomes like lamb or beef in a thick gravy. Each eater holds his bread in his hand, and piece by piece dips it in the gravy and scoops up some of the beans straight to the mouth. To accompany the *ful* everyone has a cup of black tea with a lot of sugar. Sometimes, three or four hands meet inside the bowl while dipping their bread. During the course of breakfast, the Sudanese enjoy discussing political and economic problems and their family affairs. While Nimeri was in power, opposition groups were not allowed to speak openly against the government, thus breakfast time provided the most suitable occasion to update each other on the current situation and political gossip.

Nimeri's fall was widely welcomed throughout the country by the people, as it marked the end of one and a half decades of oppressive rule. It had been a terrible experience for the freedom loving people of the Sudan.

Immediately after assuming power, President Swaradaheb

promised to hold free and fair elections within a year and hand over power to the elected representatives of the people.

The political parties banned by Nimeri re-emerged almost immediately after the change. It appeared as if the politicians had been eagerly awaiting an opportunity. All kinds of newspapers were back in circulation. The Umma Party of Sadiq al Mahdi (Ansari Sect), the National Islamic Front of Dr. Hassan Al Turabi (brother-in-law of Sadiq Al Mahdi), the Democratic Unionist Party of Al Margani and the Communist Party of Mohamed Ibrahim Nugud were the main parties in the country. They immediately set about organizing themselves for a multi-party post-Nimeri Sudan.

As Nimeri was not allowed to return home he had to stay on in Cairo where the Egyptians gave him asylum. Had he, like his predecessor Fariq Ibrahim Abbud, stepped down, bowing to the people's wishes, he could have lived in his own country. In fact, when the people compared the regime of Ibrahim Abbud with that of General Nimeri, they revised their opinion about the former and nostalgically remembered Fariq.

During the transitional year as the process of democratization gained momentum, the Sudan attracted world-wide attention. The Provisional Military regime opened the frontiers with a view to encourage the return of its nationals living abroad, many of whom were in political exile in Libya and Ethiopia. Others too returned to participate in the promised elections.

There were rumours that the returnees from Libya had brought millions of US dollars and campaign materials with them, which they were distributing among their followers to promote their prospects in the elections.

During the long dictatorship of the Nimeri regime, the people had felt suffocated. As soon as he was overthrown the new leadership allowed them full freedom. However, this also provided an opportunity to some neighbouring countries to create pockets of influence by extending support to the politicians who had found shelter in their countries and were now returning to the Sudan. Some Western countries, including the United States of America, viewed the emerging situation with concern. The US reduced the number of its diplomatic staff for security reasons. There were reports that the Western countries had advised their diplomats to restrict their movements in the country. Clearly, the diplomats from Western countries felt panicky. At cocktail parties, I heard them recalling the events of 1 March 1973 when a group of people had stormed the Embassy of Saudi Arabia in Khartoum while a cocktail party was on, and an American and a Belgian diplomat had been killed.

During this transitional period, I met leaders of various parties. As a Somali Diplomat I was interested to ascertain their position on Ethiopia vis-à-vis the Ogaden and Eritrean problems.

Sadiq Al Mahdi, the leader of the Umma Party, whom I met at his residence, did not show any interest in regional issues and was completely indifferent to what the Ethiopians were doing in their country, and to the Eritrean and the Somali struggles for the right to self-determination and independence. His attitude towards the future relationship between our two countries which in the past had been very warm, was cool.

The positions of Dr. Al Turabi of the Nationalist Islamic Front and Mr. Al Margani of the Democratic Unionist Party were, however, very clear. The two leaders, whom I visited separately, expressed their full support to the Somalis in the Ogaden. They promised that if they came to power, they would promote close cooperation in various fields between Somalia and the Sudan.

Unlike other African military leaders who had grabbed power by force, General Abdurahman Swaradaheb fulfilled his promise, handing over power to the elected leaders exactly a year later. On 6 April 1986, Sadiq Al Mahdi became Prime Minister following the victory of his Umma Party in the general elections.

I stayed on in the Sudan for only two months after Sadiq Al Mahdi assumed the premiership. Within that short period, the people had already begun agitating, raising banners with slogans such as "Nimeri come back", which had no visible impact on Nimeri's chances, but which did reveal the fickle-mindedness of the crowd mentality.

Before closing the chapter, a word about Ethiopia. Ethiopia has always had a special relationship with the Western powers and a history of collaboration with the colonialists, to the detriment of the Somalis. Moreover, Somalis have always considered

Ethiopia a colonizer, never mind that it is was an African country. It did not have a legitimate claim to the Ogaden; the Ogaden was traded by one colonial power, Britain, to another colonial power, Ethiopia. Thus, Ethiopia and Somalia seemed to be set up to ensure an unending conflict.

The Author with Tennis Trophy.

CHAPTER XIII

In Belgrade

After a short sojourn in Mogadishu, I proceeded to Belgrade to take up my new post as Ambassador to Yugoslavia in July 1986. Belgrade was a familiar city for me as I had earlier served in our embassy in that capital.

During my first short term in Belgrade in 1979, the strong man of Yugoslavia, Marshall Josip Broz Tito was firmly in the saddle. I met him once during the funeral procession of his close friend Kardel, the founder of the self-management system.

When I went to Belgrade as Ambassador of Somalia in 1986, Marshall Tito had already expired and after his death the country had switched over to a system of rotating presidents, annually appointed from among the leaders of the constituent units of the Federal Socialist Republics of Yugoslavia. Yugoslavia was composed of six republics and two autonomous provinces, and by the terms of the constitution all had equal rights.

I presented my Letters of Credence to Mr. Sinan Hassani, who was then President of the country. Mr. Hassani was from Kosovo, an autonomous province in the Republic of Serbia. The other autonomous province, also in Serbia, was Vojvodine.

According to the Constitution, the Republic of Serbia, by virtue of having two autonomous provinces, enjoyed three terms of presidency, while the other five republics had only one chance every eight years.

Relations between Somalia and Yugoslavia were cordial in general terms, but as far as Ethiopia was concerned, the Yugoslavs sympathized with the Ethiopians for various reasons of their own. Although the Ethiopian occupation of the Ogaden and Eritrea was not comparable to the nationalities problems in Yugoslavia, the Yugoslavs thought that if they supported the right to self-determination in the Horn of Africa, they might have to concede it to the people of Kosovo. Political activists from Serbia claimed that if Kosovo was made a republic, they would join neighbouring Albania.

In the autonomous province of Kosovo there were about 2 million people (about 90 percent of the total population of the province), who from time to time raised their voice against Serbian domination. Their argument was that, if Montenegro with half a million people could become a republic, why not the 2 million people of Kosovo? They were not seeking secession from the Federation, neither had they any idea of joining with Albania. According to some Kosovo politicians, the notion of secession was actually propogated by the Serbians, and then used as a pretext for maintaining their domination in the provinces. The intransigent policy of Serbia might in itself compel the Kosovos to break away.

Whilst the issue in the Horn of Africa was a question of illegal occupation of territory, the people of Kosovo were merely pleading to raise the status of their region from an autonomous province to that of a republic within the Federation. Economic cooperation between Yugoslavia and Ethiopia was very strong, whereas the cooperation between Yugoslavia and Somalia was marginal. Many Yugoslav agencies were engaged in carrying out developmental projects in Ethiopia. Even when the Yugoslavs reduced the number of scholarships to citizens of Third World countries drastically, they continued to award a good number of such scholarships to the Ethiopians.

In spite of the close and friendly relations, Yugoslavia did not openly support the Ethiopians in their dispute with us, and I did my best to maintain the cordial relations between our two countries.

Yugoslavia was a multinational country, and almost all the people of the different constituent units had maintained their identities. They prefer to be identified by their affiliations to nationalities—the Bosnians of Bosnia and Herzegovina, the Croats, the Slovenes, the Kosovos, the Serbs and the people of Montenegro. Their distinct identities on the basis of nationality divided them as sharply as tribalism and clan identities divide the Africans. The potential for breakup of the Federation has, as we have seen, become a dramatic reality since my time in Yugoslavia.

The Yugoslavs practiced a kind of discrimination against blacks, often openly. Many a cautionary tale was told in African diplomatic circles in Belgrade. Just after I had left Belgrade in 1979, an incident had occurred where a colleague of mine was beaten up with an iron bar by a Yugoslav in the heart of the city. The diplomat was badly injured but had managed to note down the number of his assailant's car. It was passed on to the Ministry of Foreign Affairs in Belgrade. A couple of years later, the Ministry replied that since the culprit had been driving a stolen car, the police had not been able to trace him. Another case involved a serious and unchecked assault by a dog on an African as he was walking along Kneiz Michailova Street in the centre of Belgrade.

In the eighties, another very serious incident, yet illustrative, occurred when an African ambassador had gone to participate in an official meeting in the capital of one of the Republics. He had gone there in his official car, driven by his chauffeur, a Yugoslav national. One morning the driver disappeared with the car. The ambassador reported the matter to the local police, who found the car rammed into a tree totally smashed, the driver having disappeared. Following his return to Belgrade by air, the Ambassador reported the matter, as procedure required, to the Ministry of Foreign Affairs. Since embassies were obliged to inform the Ministry of Foreign Affairs of the home addresses of their local employees, it was expected that the police would easily trace the delinquent driver. But this was not the case.

In some countries, the Ministry of Foreign Affairs obtains the addresses of local staff only to pass them on to their secret service to assist it in recruiting agents. Sometimes, the drivers seeking jobs in embassies are already on the secret service payroll; sometimes they are hired by the security service later. The same thing applies for secretaries and other local staff, such as messengers, cleaners and watchmen. I have had personal experience of this behaviour with a driver whom I employed in our embassy in 1979, when I was establishing the mission. He appeared very ordinary. However, I was impressed by his ability to be generally useful in solving problems that the embassy faced. His contacts in government offices were excellent and I needed a man like him at a time when we were setting up our embassy.

A few years later, when I was posted in the Sudan I came across this gentleman in Khartoum of all places.

"Hello, Excellency," he greeted me. "You remember me?" he asked. In Khartoum he was now the chauffeur of the Yugoslav Ambassador.

When I returned to Belgrade in 1986, the same man waved to me one day as I was driving to the embassy. I stopped the car to say hello to him. "Come to my office for a coffee," I said.

He expressed his delight at seeing me again. Over coffee he told me, "I am now in charge of security at the Sava Center, so if ever you need anything from there, just let me know."

Wasn't that amazing? A driver becoming the chief of security of the Sava Centre, one of the most important complexes in the city of Belgrade, and indeed in all the country!

Once, I casually remarked to a Foreign Ministry official in Belgrade that what they were doing to the African Ambassador whose car had been smashed by his driver was not proper. In a light-hearted manner I put it to him that he should concoct a story about the arrest of the driver to satisfy us, otherwise we would draw our own conclusion!

It was unbelievable that the police could fail to locate the absconding driver when a home address had been supplied to them. Besides, in Yugoslavia everything was under very tight control. Our suspicions, inevitably, were that the driver must himself have been a security officer and was being protected. Compare this incident with another in which a windscreen of a car belonging to a minor official of a European embassy was smashed, where the culprits had run away, but were apprehended by the police within a few days.

Marshall Josip Broz Tito was an extraordinarily magnetic personality, able to hold together people with distinct identities, different religions, different cultures and different languages. While he was alive, Yugoslavia was Tito and Tito was Yugoslavia.

CHAPTER XIV

The Deepening Crisis

The dictatorial regimes in both Somalia and Ethiopia were facing growing internal resistance. In Ethiopia, the Eritreans fighting for their independence achieved remarkable successes, capturing large areas of territory from Mengistu's soldiers. In 1986, Somalia presented a similarly chaotic situation. Dissidents' activities in the country and abroad were on the rise. In the northern part of the country the central government was facing a very serious threat from opposition fighting forces which had completely paralysed local administration.

Both regimes needed to re-deploy their forces to counter the growing internal resistance. Mengistu realized that his forces could not be kept in the regions bordering Somalia while he desperately needed them to fight against the Eritreans, Tigreans, and other groups who were causing him trouble in the north and east. The same was true for Mohamed Siad Barre. He needed his armed forces to fight against what he called *qaran dumiska,* the destroyers of the nation, who in this instance were his own people rather than the traditional foreign enemy, Ethiopia.

So they devised a peace formula to safeguard their own personal interests. After a relatively short period of behind-the-scenes contacts, the two leaders came to the conclusion that "peace" was essential for their two countries and peoples.

In 1986, Siad and Mengistu attended the first meeting of the Inter-Governmental Authority on Drought and Development (IGADD) held in Djibouti, and there they issued a joint statement which among other things said: "Let us spend money on tractors to help grow more food for our people instead of wasting it on armaments."

Following this meeting, and in subsequent contacts, the two countries decided to restore diplomatic relations and re-open their embassies in Mogadishu and Addis Ababa. This sudden development invited the wrath of the people of the Ogaden who were struggling for the right to self-determination, because following this agreement Mogadishu stopped supporting the liberation movements. Similarly, Mengistu also promised to stop aid to the Somali dissidents who were operating from behind what we had always regarded as artificially demarcated borders.

The Ethiopian gesture of terminating support to the Somali dissidents did not help Siad Barre very much because the dissidents continued to operate, with guerrilla tactics, from within the territory of the country.

Nor had Barre's detente with Ethiopia pleased certain groups of his erstwhile supporters, and so to try and neutralize some of the internal opposition to his recent action, and particularly to placate the Ogaden fighters, the Government coopted a number of leaders of the Western Somalia Liberation Front. For instance, a former president of the WSLF was appointed ambassador to an Arab country.

Just as Mohamed Ibrahim Egal had signed the Arusha Memorandum of Understanding with Kenya on the NFD in 1967, and Hassan Guled Abtidon and company had prevented union of the former French Somaliland with the rest in 1977, Mohamed Siad signed an agreement with Mengistu Haile Mariam abandoning the Ogaden in 1986. In short, by 1986 the Somali leaders had unofficially and indirectly renounced all claim to our 'missing territories'.

Recent events in the Horn has brought new leaders to Ethiopia, leaders who were supported in their struggle by the Somali people. We are hopeful that our brothers who were subjugated by the earlier tyrannical Ethiopian regimes may now expect justice.

Meanwhile, for the common people in Somalia by the late eighties, the struggle for survival had become acute. A large majority of civil servants, whose average income was less than US $5.00 a month, were forced to seek additional private work to cope with the burden imposed by growing inflation. Absenteeism in Government offices increased even further. The system was on the verge of collapse. Corruption and malpractices had come full circle from the eve of the military coup in 1969.

While the masses were suffering greatly, the ruling elite and the members of the upper stratum of the population were leading an extravagant, luxurious life. They had everything in abundance. Water and diesel were scarce commodities for the common man but the tanks of the rich were always full. The women in high society competed with each other to acquire the newest model of car to add to the collection in their garages. Possession of a Landcruiser was a special status symbol for those families who were members of the ruling clan. Their teenage children indulged in racing sprees, chasing one another through the narrow lanes of the city in their 'toy' automobiles. It was not uncommon for them to brandish pistols and begin shooting into the air. And why not? It was fun, and they could afford it.

In 1986, driving from the town of Afgoye to the capital, President Siad had a car accident. Badly injured, he was rushed to the best hospital in the country—the Police Force Hospital—the one with a wing reserved for Central Committee Members of the ruling Somali Revolutionary Socialist Party (SRSP).

When he arrived at the hospital he was unconscious. After 17 years of his rule, the best hospital in the country did not even have oxygen to help him return to consciousness. An emergency call was made to Kenya, a neighbour with whom our relations had always been difficult. Nevertheless, an ambulance plane with doctors on board was immediately sent from Nairobi. A second call was made to Saudi Arabia, and the King also ordered the immediate despatch of a special aircraft and doctors. Finally, the President was flown to Saudi Arabia. On arrival at Riyadh Hospital he was taken to the Intensive Care Unit. The President of the Republic could not be treated in his own country, the country whose welfare and progress had been in his hands for 17 years.

Those who knew the real condition of the country were not at all surprised. Our hospitals were poorly maintained, and life-saving drugs and equipment were either in short supply or were not available at all. If this was the medical situation in the capital, what could one expect in the interior of the country? The common man, of course, knew all this, could die in agony and nobody would notice. But our leaders did not need to bother themselves with the poor conditions in our hospitals because they rarely used them. Whenever they or their families required medical attention they went abroad at the nation's expense.

If the first decade of the Revolution had seen some tangible achievements, the second decade, since the Ogaden War, had reflected deterioration and decline in every sector of national life.

In the 1970s, when Somalia had been a model for centralized development strategies, and had been host to countless State visitors and delegates to international meetings, the capital Mogadishu had the reputation for being the cleanest city and, security-wise, the safest in the region. But the city which had once been described as 'the pearl of the Indian Ocean' had been reduced to the dirtiest and darkest city.

After treatment and recuperation which lasted a couple of months, President Siad returned to Mogadishu and resumed his duties. Physically, he was not as robust as he had once been, and the mental shock caused by the accident had also left him apparently hesitant.

When the President met with his accident in 1986 he was officially 67 years old, and for his age he was strong, fit and had tremendous stamina. But after the accident, he looked much older and weaker. Almighty Allah was very generous, however. He had saved his life. Probably, Allah wanted him to repent for his vanity and excesses, and ask for forgiveness. As in 1977, the best course of action would have been for him to abdicate the Presidency, this time on health grounds. His image was already tarnished severely, and there was ever-increasing corruption and deterioration in the law and order situation.

In the years since 1977, President Barre had shuffled and re-shuffled his Government with cosmetic effect. Those who were inducted into or removed were always the same old faces. Even after dismissal from their ministerial posts, they were treated like 'ministers without portfolio', allowed to keep their official houses, cars, and house staff, continuing to enjoy their ministerial privileges. Most of them were sacked and re-appointed several times over the years. One of the reasons why mistakes could never be corrected was this lack of real change in the personnel of the leadership. These cosmetic re-shufflings of the cabinet further undermined the legitimacy of the entire leadership, including that of President Barre.

In private, some Ministers had started criticising the President for his lack of trust in them. Their anger and frustration was fuelled by the President's increasing fondness for appointing and deputing members of his own clan in various ministries, to oversee the activities of his own ministers. In due course of time, these Presidential appointees came to exercise more power and influence than the ministers themselves.

The President's appointees were particularly in evidence in departments dealing with finance and development projects. It was said that they had been posted there to make a quick fortune. They worked, for instance, as brokers and middlemen at customs, and at the revenue collection departments of municipalities. Consequently, no one paid into the State treasury; everything was bargained and settled outside the State machinery.

As a result, the ruling clan found itself isolated from all the other clans, including those which were tribally close to them.

The public stopped depositing their money in the banks, because they believed that depositors' money was being given to people bringing recommendation letters from the President for 'bank loans'. Hundreds of millions of shillings were being borrowed from the banks without guarantees. Consequently, the public decided not to put their money in the banks any more. It was time for the President to step in. He addressed a large public gathering and said that the Government could not be held responsible for the loss of any sums of money the people kept in their houses, instead of depositing in the banks. Inevitably, this was interpreted as a license for domestic robbery.

Many people found that their bank deposits had disappeared. Those who owed banks large sums could bribe bankers to destroy records so that they could escape repayment of massive debts. The country's banking system had collapsed.

Soon after the President's speech, the incidence of theft and burglary sure enough showed a phenomenal increase. Preposterous as it appeared, trained thieves made use of their Landcruisers to wrench out the steel doors of shops in the city.

The people's reluctance to deposit their money in banks led to a new crisis. The banks ceased to have enough liquid cash and were forced to adopt a policy of 'rationing', or restricting the amount a depositor could encash each day. For some families, the amount was barely enough for one meal. Rich men cried out: "I have millions in my account but cannot even withdraw enough of my own money to feed my family."

The situation was impossible for the city dwellers. The banks were only kept open because the Government did not want to declare a state of bankruptcy.

There was also an extreme shortage of currency notes, obliging a large number of people in the city to use cheques—not a common or usual method of transacting business in Mogadishu—for the purchase of consumer items. Then, the value of cheques in the market declined. Shopkeepers or moneybrokers accepted them only at a discount, which ranged from 20 to 30 per cent. The rate of discount was higher during the weekends and on the eve of holidays. All such transactions were illegal. But sometimes even government departments made use of the new system.

The growing economic and political problems further eroded the position and authority of President Siad. Some of his old colleagues and friends were emboldened enough to blame him, by inference, for the problems the country faced. At the weekly meeting of the Council of Ministers, chaired by himself, the President would raise such innocent questions as: What is wrong with the people? What is the problem? What do they want? To which a member of the civilian segment of the cabinet might timorously reply: We are the problem. If we go, the situation will improve. But the former members of the Revolutionary Council, soldiers to a man, who had been instrumental in staging the coup would say that they had personally risked their lives during the coup. While their civilian colleagues had been asleep, they had taken over power with the help of the gun and by the gun alone would somebody take it from them.

In the northern part of the country, the Somali National Movement, consisting of former Ministers, retired and defecting diplomats and civil servants, as well as Army officers who had defected from the Revolutionary regime, was waging a violent struggle against the armed forces loyal to President Siad.

In 1988, our self-styled *Aabaahii Ummadda Soomaaliyeed*, Father of the Somali Nation, ordered the airforce and artillery to bombard the city of Hargeisa—the second capital of the country—and Burao city, both in the north, forcing their inhabitants to flee to the countryside or across to neighbouring Ethiopia. There were rumours that he had hired South African mercenaries to fly the MIG jet fighters that mercilessly bombarded these cities. This may not be as unbelievable as it sounds, since a team of white South African pilots and technicians was working with the Somali MIG pilots based in Baidoa.

The airforce and the artillery left not a single building, not even a mosque, untouched. The troops then mined the whole city and its surroundings, to destroy and deter returning citizens. Yet, the Somali National Movement continued its fight against the regime. The people's anger and hurt was too deep.

In Mogadishu, a popular joke which reflected the desperate situation in the country, went something like this:

The President called for his barber, a Reer Hamar, to dress his hair. While the barber was doing his job the following conversation took place between them.

Barber: Aabe Siad, may I ask a question, Sir?

President: Yes, what is it?

Barber: What's all the excitement in the countryside?

President: You Hamaris never understand anything. It's just the regional games. What else did you think?

Barber: Oh, very interesting. Then aren't the finals going to be in the capital?

As his position weakened, Siad Barre surrounded himself with his close relatives, appointing them to all the important posts. During this difficult period in the history of our country, the frequency of foreign tours by the relatives of Siad, and by his ministers, increased sharply. Some of them bought houses or apartments in Western countries and settled there.

With every passing day, tensions in the country increased. The Government was facing massive opposition, both from within and outside the country. There was a resurgence of political activities. As there were no traditional places for political meetings, people started organizing themselves in the mosques, specially on Fridays. The Government tried to intimidate the religious elements and described them in derogatory terms as fundamentalists. Some of them were called in by the Security Service for daily interrogation. Undaunted by the Government policy of intimidation, the religious groups continued to send secret messages to be delivered in mosques on Fridays throughout the country.

In 1989 Monsignor Colombo, the chief priest of the Roman Catholic Church of Mogadishu was gunned down in the grounds of the cathedral, and the killer escaped. The Government announced a reward of five million Somali shillings for information on the killer. It appeared to the people that the Government gave more value to the life of one 'unbeliever' than to the many Somalis who were dying daily at the hands of criminals or the security forces.

In reaction to the Government's offer, an underground organization in the capital announced a reward of 10 million Somali Shillings for information on whoever claimed the Government reward.

Father Colombo had been in the country for over forty years. Many international organizations considered him an expert on Somali affairs. Though the leaders did not go to the Church for confession, Padre Colombo was believed to have known all their sins. The motives and the identity of the assassin(s) of Bishop Colombo have still not been established.

The reaction of the Security Service was to arrest a number of religious people on suspicion, accusing them of fanaticism or fundamentalism. Appeals to the Government for their release went unheeded. So, religious groups decided to organize a peaceful demonstration in support of the arrested people. The demonstration was to be held on Friday, following the main midday prayers at the mosque. The Government, however, received information about the plan and decided to suppress it by force. Accordingly, on 14 July 1989, the Security Forces armed with automatic weapons surrounded the main mosques in the capital, including the Mosque of Shaikh Ali Sufi. A large number of people had come to offer prayers at this Mosque. Except for the old and infirm who were carrying their walking sticks, most of the worshippers were unarmed. Yet, they were ready to face the guns. Immediately after the prayers, the people began shouting, "*Allahu Akbar*", "*Allahu Akbar*", (God is Great, God is Great).

As soon as they came out of the Mosques, they were met with bullets from automatic weapons. Many fell, others of the crowd dispersed helter-skelter in different directions. The provocation by the soldiers heightened the resolve of some protesters. Mayhem raged in the streets for several hours. Houses in the Hodan and Casa Popolare areas of the city were searched at gunpoint and families terrorised and intimidated by the soldiers. What happened on that day was a nightmare for the residents of Mogadishu.

Despite the firing, the people continued their protests with greater determination and vigour. The sound of the bullets could be heard around the city, like rain, falling on corrugated iron roofs. An unknown number of people were either killed or injured on that day. That day, when Muslims all over the world were observing their holy day, the Government in Somalia was once again brutally killing its own people.

In Somalia it seemed that the lives of human beings had no value at all—that every other thing had become expensive except for life. Shortly after the Mosque shootings, another horrifying event, the massacre of 41 men at the beach of Jesira, 14 kilometers from Mogadishu, took place. The victims, sleeping in their homes, were rounded up at about three in the morning by gunmen who took them away in two waiting lorries. Indiscriminate arrests had become common practice. The victims might optimistically have thought they were being forcibly conscripted, and being taken to the nearby military training camp at Dhanaane. Residents in the neighbourhood, hearing a commotion, were unlikely to brave coming out of their houses to check what was going on.

The people arrested did not offer any resistance because their captors were well armed. They were driven towards Jesira which was in the same direction as the Dhanaane military camp, but they did not suspect foul play. However, this time it was to be quite different. After passing Jesira village, the lorries stopped in the middle of nowhere and unloaded 'the passengers' who were ordered to sit on the sand and put their hands behind their heads. The gunmen opened fire, massacring all.

After the mass killing, the victims were buried under the sand. The gunmen hurriedly left the scene of the crime, but unknowingly, they had left one lucky victim still alive. Though injured he had feigned dead, and after the killers had left emerged from the sandy mass grave. After washing the blood and sand off himself in the sea nearby, he started back on foot to the city.

He reported to his brother-in-law, a high-ranking official, what had happened to the others. The brother-in-law in turn rushed to the politbureau member in charge of National Security—himself the son-in-law of the President. Along with a few elders of the capital, he approached the President to inform him of the ghastly killings. The President is reported to have refused to believe the story. In any case, as there was no accountability, nobody was brought to book. Young men of certain tribal affiliations could not sleep safely in their own beds, and shifted every night to relatives with neutral-clan or ruling-clan connections for protection.

This horrific incident, ghastly as it was, was only indicative of the wretchedness of life in Somalia, and something had to break. President Siad Barre had long since lost touch with the people. Work in Government Ministries and offices had come to a grinding halt. There was no stationery, type writers were put aside for lack of paper and ribbon, people printed their own official letterheads on which they typed official letters and they made the rubber stamps they needed to authenticate these documents.

Somalia had developed a do-it-yourself survival strategy. The Government had become an irrelevance.

CHAPTER XV

The Manifesto

In May 1990, a group of businessmen, intellectuals, professionals and politicians appealed to the President to resign so that the country could be saved. They sent him a memorandum—'Manifesto Numero Uno' signed by 114 persons, on 15 May 1990. Among other things, it proposed that 13 of the signatories be nominated to an interim council to run the country until elections were held. The significance of some aspects of the presentation of the Manifesto were not lost on those who understood the situation, for example:

There are 114 *suras* in the Koran.

15 May was the foundation date of the Somali Youth Club which later became the Somali Youth League—the main party of the independence movement.

There were 13 founding members of the SYC.

I was then in Mogadishu on a short visit following my father's death which had occurred a few days before. The whole city was talking about the Manifesto. People were wondering what would happen to the signatories who included national luminaries and personalities such as Aden Abdulle Osman the first President, Ismail Jimale, Ali Mahdi, Ibrahim Abyan 'Madoowbe' and many others of note.

My conjecture was that Siad himself had asked the elders to send to him such a memorandum, and intended it for his own use or purpose—perhaps to use it as an excuse to resign, on the pretext that he had been asked by the elders to hand over power to them, or to gain time, or to come up with new ideas. He was a wily fox, capable of anything. During those days, Siad held frequent meetings with various politicians who were advising him to relinquish his position and save the country from total disaster.

It did seem to me, however, that there were only two possible outcomes: one, was that he would relinquish power as proposed by the Manifesto, or two, that he would hold on to power and order the arrest of all the signatories of the Memorandum on the grounds that they were all corrupt people whom he had toppled in the Revolution and who were creating trouble in order to regain power.

However, it was not really such a straightforward choice. Past experience should have warned us that he would never resign. He had not relinquished power on two previous occasions for the sake of the unity, integrity and peace of the country, so why should he do so now? The first time, he might have resigned and been considered a hero; the second time, his accident might have earned him some public sympathy. Now, it was difficult to see how he could salvage anything positive of his personal legacy. Regarding the alternative of arresting the authors of the Manifesto, it became suddenly clear that the Revolution had no teeth left for such action. Not only were the Somalis pressing him to go. Countries considered friendly towards him, like the USA, Italy and Egypt, were also impressing upon him the need to let the people organize themselves, and to this end they offered their good offices to mediate between him and the opposition groups. But Siad Barre refused to listen to anybody.

Somalis all over the country were praying for his removal from power by one means or another, and to see an end to his tyrannical rule which had become intolerable.

On 2 June, the Italian Embassy held a reception to celebrate its national day. The Italian Ambassador, I suppose with the full knowledge and consent of his Government, invited all the signatories and promoters of Manifesto Numero Uno to attend. When the regime came to know of the invitations, it ordered the Security Service to stop all Somalis except for Ministers from entering the Italian Embassy. The Security people entered the embassy with walkie-talkies and placed plain-clothed personnel at both gates of the premises.

The Manifesto Group anticipated their arrests, but were prepared to face any consequences. By attending the reception, they would be challenging the President, who could retaliate harshly. Many of the group were well aware of conditions in prison, they having already been there as political prisoners of Siad.

At the rear entrance to the embassy, the guards did not stop anyone. At the front, the Police and Security stopped everybody. They had been told by their superiors that only the Ministers should be permitted to enter. Interpreting the order literally to mean that only Wazirs could pass, they tried to prevent Ministers of State and Vice Ministers, and other senior officials such as directors general from entering the embassy. However, since neither the security officers nor the police seemed able to recognize by face the different personalities, and in spite of their best bungled efforts, Security failed to stop the Manifesto people from attending the Reception.

The Italian Ambassador was annoyed at what the Somali Government had done. His guests were also highly critical of the security officers' behaviour.

The Americans and Italians who were hosting opposition groups in their countries, were trying to persuade Siad Barre to emerge from the crisis peacefully. Eventually, he agreed to send a delegation to Cairo, to participate in a meeting with representatives of opposition groups, and with Egypt and Italy mediating. But, just before the departure of the delegation to the Egyptian capital, most of the Manifesto Group were arrested. While some blamed the President for ordering their arrest, others thought they had been arrested at the behest of some of the President's men who were opposed to any meeting with the opposition groups.

Conflicting reports were circulating in the capital about the President's willingness to relinquish power. Some held that whereas he was willing to hand over to the President of the National Assembly and pave the way for a transition, his family and friends were dissuading him from doing so because they anticipated adverse consequences for their own future positions. Meanwhile, the nation eagerly awaited his response to The Manifesto.

In July 1990, President Siad Barre appeared on national television to address the nation on the occasion of Eid Al Adha. The Government generally used such occasions as Independence Day, Eid al Fitr or Eid al Adha to announce reprieves and amnesties to political prisoners. Therefore, the people expected such an overture from the President, as a gesture of reconciliation with the proposers of reform.

Contrary to all such expectations, the President announced that the signatories of the Manifesto belonged to the former corrupt regime which the Revolution had toppled, and he had decided to put them on trial before a special court.

Whoever it was who had advised him on such a confrontational course had set him on a difficult path, which was neither in his interest nor in the interest of the nation.

I had been appointed Ambassador to the Republic of India in June 1989. Besides India, I am also accredited to the Republic of Sri Lanka and the Republic of Singapore. This is my third consecutive posting as Ambassador.

I invited the Somalis living in India to the embassy for an informal get-together. I told them that the embassy would do everything to help them, and advised them to form an association, with representatives who could come to the embassy to discuss their problems. Besides students, there was also a small community of Somalis resident in Delhi.

We were there to help them as much as we could. Their main problem has always related to passports. In the past, the embassy has exempted full-time students from paying Consular fees. But, later in the revolutionary era, the Government changed the rules and instructed embassies to charge fees of everyone, including students. In 1989, the Government decided to change all passports, and instructed all embassies to charge US $100.00 instead of US $20.00, to be paid in American dollars. The circular instructing the embassies was signed by the President himself and not by the Minister of Foreign Affairs or by the Director in charge of passports. The instruction also stipulated that the fees received from the passports should be remitted to an account in a Bank in Dubai, in the United Arab Emirates.

It was unusual for us to send State funds to a bank in the UAE. In the past we had sent revenues to the Ministry of Foreign Affairs, and in turn the Ministry sent it to the Revenue Office. As soon as the embassy received the President's circular I wrote to the Ministry emphasizing the need to make an exception for students, who should either have their fee waived or reduced. The fees proposed in the circular were in any case five times higher than those being charged in Mogadishu. It was, moreover, illegal in India as elsewhere for people to transact in foreign currency outside the banking system.

Until a reply to my letter was received the embassy had to follow instructions. However, we decided to charge the fees in local currency instead of US dollars, which would be very difficult for the students to obtain.

In May 1990, while in Mogadishu, I called on the President as was usual. After briefing him on the general situation in the country I was accredited to, I mentioned the new rules on passport fees which I had been trying to convince the authorities to amend.

"Go and speak to the Minister of Finance," he said to me. I told him that since his signature was on the circular, the Finance Minister was likely to send me back to him.

He was wearing dark glasses and I could not see his eyes. I had known him since 1972, when I first met him in China on his official visit there, but had never found him so indifferent to matters. I was sitting in front of him in his small office in the villa which the Italians had called La Foresteria. I was wondering whether he realized he had signed the circular or not. In the last few years, it was said, his trusted advisors were misusing his confidence in them.

"O.K. See me before you return to India," he said.

I went to see him again at the beginning of July 1990, three days before my departure for New Delhi. He was sitting in the garden where he generally received visitors. I sat down and told him I was ready to return to my post. I reminded him that I was waiting for an answer about the passport fees. He had not remembered, as there were so many other serious problems he was faced with. When I repeated what I had said, he asked me what I thought. I said that I favoured a uniform rate for all nationals, at home or abroad. I knew that every Somali who lived abroad was not rich. Many of them could barely afford their daily food. He agreed that, until I received further instructions I should collect the fees at the rate being charged in Mogadishu. I do not know why I bothered, because each embassy apparently did what it wanted, but it is my way to establish and follow procedures.

That was the last time I met President Siad. I had found him a changed man. Once, he used to crack jokes and engage in lively repartee with his guests. Now he appeared preoccupied, or to have lost interest. Once he functioned as a leader with authority. However, in his final years he delegated power to those from whom he could strip it most easily. He was weak, and those he trusted were also so weak that they could not even control their messengers.

Finally, what happened to him is best expressed in the Somali proverb which says:

Nin liita har kuuma jiido
A weak person cannot carry you to the shade.

CHAPTER XVI

The End of a Dream

1990 was a very crucial year for Somalia. It was clear to every sensible person that the country would either be plunged into civil war or a solution to the problem of the President would have to be found. Meanwhile, to sustain himself in power he was repeatedly changing prime ministers, and ultimately promised constitutional reforms to include the introduction of a multi-party system.

The Presidential armed guards continued to harass the people, indulging in criminal acts of robbery and killing of innocent people. Violence gradually engulfed the entire country.

The barber's joke about the finals being played out in the capital was proving prophetic. A number of armed groups sneaked into the capital, carrying heavy machine guns, artillery pieces and even rocket launchers.

As the opposition forces seemed to have gained the upper hand over what could be termed the President's 'private troops', comprising as they did his own tribesmen, he called for a ceasefire and offered negotiations. In 1988 he had been able to hire South African mercenary pilots to destroy the second capital of the Republic and other parts of the Northern Region. Towards the end of his reign, he enjoyed the support of only his tribal forces, all others having already abandoned him. The opposition groups rejected his offer of negotiations and insisted on his removal from the Somali political scene. By this stage the entire population of the country supported the opposition. All the President's supporters, except his family, deserted him and were fleeing the country in search of safety.

Yet, he stubbornly refused to heed the advice of friendly countries, the growing demands of the people and the appeals of the elders to relinquish power. With bravado, he threatened he would fight to hold on to the last inch of territory. He said that if the opposition captured the Kaaraan District of the capital, he

would withdraw to Bondhere District. He would never sur-
render, whatever the consequences. On Sunday, 30, December
1990, the opposition forces in the capital launched a major assault on various positions and bases of the Government.

Siad Barre's generals had informed him that the opposition
guerrillas were equipped with only a few light armaments.
When he heard the sound of heavy shells falling nearby, he knew
what kind of guns were actually being fired. He is reported to
have said to the trusties who were with him "Why did you tell me
they had only small guns?"

He brought reinforcements of loyal troops from the interior,
but they could not help him. In the midst of the fighting, which
continued for several days, the elders tried to work out a
ceasefire, to give him an opportunity to abdicate.

Finally, about a month later, on the evening of January 27,
1991, a Sunday, President Mohamed Siad Barre fled in disgrace
from the Presidency—the *Madaxtooyada*—hidden in a military
tank. It was the finals of the Regional Games, and Siad's team
lost.

Postscript

All over the country there was enthusiastic support for the struggle to overthrow the regime because, except for Siad Barre's close relatives and friends, everyone had suffered one way or another under his tyrannical rule.

The opposition movements, promising justice, equality and democracy, took over the country. Mohamed Siad Barre was compelled to flee the capital, driven out by forces of the United Somali Congress (USC). In the North the Somali National Movement (SNM) liquidated the remnants of his regime from the region.

The leaders who took over power in Mogadishu without prior consultation with the different groups who had fought against the regime of Siad Barre, unexpectedly and unilaterally appointed Ali Mahdi Mohamed, a prominent businessman, as interim president.

Bearing in mind the nature of the struggle an armed struggle which had been waged by various groups for longer or shorter periods of time it was an immature step not to consult. Consequently, most of the neglected groups raised their voices against this hasty decision.

To calm down the popular protest, the interim President proposed to convene an all-party conference to discuss the situation. Almost all the main organized groups rejected the proposal and demanded his resignation. Meanwhile, the fighting which had engulfed the capital in the final days of Siad continued unabated, and the self-appointed interim government was unable to stop it. People who were suspected of having connections with the tribe of Siad were hounded and killed. The violence degenerated into anarchy.

Armed desperados unleashed an unimaginable spectacle of mass killing and destruction on the city. Life became brutal, short and nasty. People began fleeing for their lives to the countryside, some attempting to get to the safety of their tribal homelands, others to different towns and, if they did not find any escape from violence there either, were rushing back towards the capital.

Those who could manage to were fleeing to the neighbouring countries of Kenya and Ethiopia, on foot, by car, and by sea in small fishing boats. They did so at great risk; in one incident alone, hundreds of them were drowned when the overloaded boat they were escaping in capsized off the Kenyan coast near Mombasa.

In the face of all this trouble the Government of Ali Mahdi could not make its presence felt. It issued a decree calling upon the people to return all looted State property to the Government store. Culprits not heeding the call were threatened with long-term imprisonment. The decree also called on those who had illegally occupied houses of other people to vacate them immediately. But to no avail.

While retreating from the capital, Mohamed Siad Barre's soldiers destroyed whatever they could on their way to the interior part of the country, which was their tribal homeland. The resistance groups which had replaced the Siad regime in the southern part of the country failed to discipline their fighters and restore law and order. The resistance groups in the north were more successful in bringing about a domestic calm, and families who had fled from Siad's repression to refugee camps in Ethiopia began returning home, hoping to re-build their lives.

In Mogadishu, hooligans and anarchists went on a looting spree. They spared nothing, whether banks, government offices, schools, or private houses. Since they had no value, bundles of currency notes were thrown on the streets, as were office documents. Typewriters, chairs, tables, and anything else of value were stolen.

In our collective anger, we did not differentiate between the national property and the property of the individuals who had held power and against whom our anger was being vented. Instead of protecting State property as national assets, we recklessly destroyed it as if it were the property of our enemies.

It is well-known that Mohamed Siad Barre played one clan against the other in order to rule over all. But the opposition, which forced him to run away, itself continued his evil designs. People had a right to expect that after his departure a new

leadership would make attempts to resolve the problems afflict-
ing the nation in a democratic manner, but their hopes were
belied.

The leaders have failed to formulate a coherent policy. There
is no consensus among them on the form of administration they
should adopt. Individuals are busy promoting their own selfish
interests at the cost of the indescribable suffering of the people.

On 18 May 1991, the Somali National Movement in the north
of the country declared its independence from Mogadishu, and
proclaimed the formation of what it called 'the Republic of
Somaliland'. The Somali National Movement refused to attend
the reconciliation talks held in Djibouti in June, stating that 'The
Republic of Somaliland' would deal with the South as a neighbouring state.

Since 1960, when former British Somaliland and former
Italian Somalia united as one country, they had kept the candle
burning for the eventual freedom and unification of all Somalis.
With the recent secession of the northern region, and the
celebration in 1991 of a separate Independence Day by northern
Somalia, the Somalis' national dream of uniting the five Somali
regions under one flag lay totally shattered.

It is truly ironic and indeed tragic that, if the policies of our
colonial masters are compared with those pursued by our own
leaders, we are left with serious disappointments, and a
catalogue of missed opportunities and lost chances. We have
committed atrocities—untold atrocities—against ourselves. It
was the colonialist, Mr. Bevin, who once advocated the cause of
uniting all the Somalis into a Greater Somaliland. Yet our
leaders, since independence in 1960, successively, either gave
away or created conditions to divide all the territories which we
claimed ours.

The most unfortunate part of the story is that Somalia has
failed to produce honest leaders. Our leaders have been selfish
and avaricious, even embezzling and misappropriating the
meagre assistance given to us by our friends and former colonial
powers. We were always ready to hurl abuse on outsiders for the
sad plight in which we found ourselves, and much of the blame is
well-placed. But do we ever dare admit our own mistakes or
evaluate our history objectively? In the five decades of the his-

tory of our statehood which is covered in my narrative we have travelled a road which had brought us down to zero.

The Siad regime perpetrated a reign of oppression, especially during the second half of its 21 year rule. Must his successors repeat what he did to the people and country, or should they try to heal the wounds that his regime has inflicted on us? Have we given due thought to where the policy of vengeance and fratricidal action will lead us?

Yet, we are still engaged in a relentless power struggle. In spite of the fact that hundreds of thousands of people have been killed in this power struggle we have still not learnt anything. Unless the warring groups can agree that all must participate in power-sharing, in a democratic way, there cannot be any peace. If today, one group usurps power through violence, another group will certainly do the same tomorrow.

Somalia, almost two years from the ousting of Siad, presents a picture of a battlefield—dead bodies lying in the streets, the injured, disabled and maimed crying for mercy.

In the violent fighting between the rival groups, which took place in Mogadishu in the latter half of November 1991, thousands are reported to have died, most of them innocent civilians, children and women caught in the crossfire.

Dr. Sam Toussie, one of the medical doctors sent by the International Committee of the Red Cross, described the situation in Mogadishu in the following chilling words:

'I have been in wars for eight years, and I have never seen a slaughter like this. We were getting 150 casualties a day at one hospital. Seventy five per cent were children and we were losing five persons an hour. We had parents coming into the hospital compound armed.'

In its Press Release on 29 November, 1991, the International Committee of the Red Cross said:

'The situation in Somalia is a human disaster of the first magnitude. Fighting continues unabated in Mogadishu with heavy shelling and continuous gun fire.

'There are thousands of wounded, including many women and children. Large numbers of them are not treated in hospital because of lack of security and the impossibility of transferring them. The medical infrastructure is quite inadequate to cope with the extreme emergency of the situation.'

The Press Release concluded by appealing to the rival groups to take all possible measures to facilitate the work of relief workers and medical teams in Mogadishu and to help in evacuating the wounded.

All those who have wished to leave their names in history and who have only used force to achieve it, have created misery for millions in the lands they have governed. Only a small plot of land 6ft x 2ft finally belonged to them by right. And some recent dictators have even been denied little graves in their homelands.

An Indian Professor friend remarked to me recently, "Tyrants have come and tyrants have gone. The power of the ruler comes from the people and when the ruler forgets the source of his power and thinks it is inherent in him, he becomes a tyrant, eventually to be crushed by the source of his own power."

Mengistu is gone. Siad is gone. Ceaucescu of Romania toppled and killed. Earlier the Shah of Iran had to leave, and Iddi Amin of Uganda. Marcos of the Philippines too is gone. Any leader who follows their example will do so to the final chilling end.

Even if any of the rival groups wins the genocidal war in my country, it is likely to result in a re-emergence of tyrannical dictatorship, the survival of which will be dependent on brute power rather than the free will of the people.

Is there no escape for us from this purgatory? Are we destined to play this barbaric game until we all perish? Oh Allah, have mercy upon us. If what is happening in my country is divine punishment, we pray You to test us no more, and help us instead to reorganize our national life in a peaceful way. Amen.

Index